The Prison Path

The Prison Path

School Practices that Hurt Our Youth

Christen E. Clemson

ROWMAN & LITTLEFIELD
Lanham • Boulder • New York • London

Published by Rowman & Littlefield
A wholly owned subsidiary of The Rowman & Littlefield Publishing Group, Inc.
4501 Forbes Boulevard, Suite 200, Lanham, Maryland 20706
www.rowman.com

Unit A, Whitacre Mews, 26-34 Stannary Street, London SE11 4AB

British Library Cataloguing in Publication Information Available

Library of Congress Cataloging-in-Publication Data Available

ISBN 978-1-61048-979-9 (cloth)
ISBN 978-1-61048-980-5 (pbk.)
ISBN 978-1-61048-981-2 (electronic)

Contents

Preface

In the 2012–2013 school year, the United States spent approximately 11,810 dollars per student on education.[1] At the same time, federal prison expenditures per inmate were 26,359 dollars annually.[2] This gross discrepancy between schools and prisons is problematic; prisons are the schools for those whom school fails. Without casting blame, this book attempts to explore the similarities between schools and prisons and to bring awareness to those within both institutions. Every student who can be kept in school is one less person likely to be incarcerated.

The idea for the research and book began during a conversation with a friend. This friend had trained as a teacher, but had difficulty finding a permanent position. After several years of substitute teaching, he took a position as a "teacher" in a school for troubled youth. He once told me that his time at this school consisted of breaking up fights and keeping the peace; little traditional teaching actually occurred. When a position as a correctional officer opened in a federal correctional institution, he applied for and received the job.

As I was looking for a topic to research in an ethics class, he mentioned to me the similarities he had seen during his time as a teacher and his current position as a correctional officer. At first, I laughed, thinking that he was joking and attempting to relieve stress after a rough day. However, he continued on the topic, speaking about how the bell system in the prison mirrored the bell system of the schools, how the discipline strategies were similar, and the groups of people he dealt with were analogous.

While he was speaking, the ramifications of what he was saying finally infiltrated my mind: What if prisons were more similar to schools than anyone wanted to imagine? What if schools who failed students were creating a class of students more likely to go to prison than to college? What other structures were similar between schools and prisons? These questions began my seven-year quest into the research of schools and prisons.

Diving into this research, I immediately hit a problem; there was hardly any existing research on the topic. Yes, research on the school-to-prison pipeline was prevalent and relevant, but nothing discussed the similarity in the structures of schools and prisons. Research on the pipeline examines practices and policies that funnel mostly Black and Hispanic male youth from schools into prisons. Pipeline research examines policies like zero tolerance, special education, and discipline strategies, not the structural similarities of the two institutions.

In my research pursuits, I have stumbled on some research gems and unlikely supporters, but I have run across an equal amount of criticism and cynics. In fact, one professor flat-out told me that my idea was ludicrous and not worth my time or energy. It was neither the first nor the last time I encountered such criticism. However, the vast majority of teachers and practitioners that I have spoken with immediately relate, understand, and agree with many points and comparisons.

This research is neither complete nor perfect, but it is profound and startling. I hope that as you read this book, you will examine your practices with an eye toward improvement, better policy creation, and implementing fundamental change that will improve education for all students. We are doing the best we can with what we are currently given, but it is time that we as teachers and administrators demand better resources, more funding, and the prestige that we deserve to help all students find their inner strengths and lifelong success.

NOTES

1. National Center for Education Statistics. (2013). *Fast Facts*. Retrieved from: http://nces.ed.gov/fastfacts/display.asp?id=372

2. Bureau of Prisons. (2012), *Federal Prison System per Capita Costs*, Retrieved from: http://www.bop.gov/foia/fy12_per_capita_costs.pdf

Acknowledgments

This book truly would not have been possible without my amazing mother. When I came home from a conference and told her Nancy Evans from Rowan and Littlefield had approached me to write a book, my mother encouraged me to take the leap. She spent long hours helping me formulate ideas, talking through situations, proofreading, and sharing her knowledge. Thank you, Mom, for your love, support, and patience throughout the years. Secondly, this book would not exist without my brother. I love you, I am so proud of you, and I am so grateful you are my family. A huge thank goes out to my grandparents, Mary and Joe Letwen, for their love, support, and unwavering faith throughout the years, as well as my grandmother, Betty Clemson.

My deepest appreciation goes out to Nancy Evans. Without her, this book would not exist. She believed in my message, my voice, and convinced me that I had the courage to write down what I knew. I must also thank Joy Meness (and her daughter, Nicole) for our daily coffee dates on my couch and walks. Without your point of view and insights, these ideas might never have seen the light of day. I would also like to thank my graduate school friends, Shelly, Jeannette, and Hend. You have kept me sane and motivated. In addition, a giant thank you goes out to the Patio Party Group! There really are not words to describe our conversations, laughter, and friendship.

Finally, yet importantly, I would like to thank Dr. Paul Begley, Dr. Jacqueline Stefkovich, Dr. Anthony Normore. Dr. Begley, my first mentor, you introduced me to the world of academia and taught me to stand up for what I believed in, and I am fortunate enough to be able to count you as a friend. Dr. Jacqueline Stefkovich, my current mentor, has guided me through the pitfalls of research and academia, bravely supporting me through this rocky journey of discovery. Without her, the idea for this book would never have existed. I would also like to thank Dr. Normore. You have been a wonderful guide, supporter, and voice of experience. Your help has been treasured.

Lastly, I would like to thank all my friends and family not mentioned. All of you have listened to me complain, groan, rejoice, cite random statistics, and solicit stories as I have made my way through chapters of this book. I thank you all for your patience and your sharing. I am truly blessed to have the best family and friends ever. Thank you all.

Foreword

Anthony H. Normore, Ph.D, California State University Dominguez Hills

National figures suggest that millions of students are at risk of dropping out of school. Data further reveals that "many of these students come from groups that are underserved and underrepresented: students of color, high-mobility students (including foster, migrant and homeless), English language learners, students with disabilities and low-income students (Esposito & Normore, in press). Although progress has been made in advancing equity agendas of access, participation, and academic achievement for individuals with disabilities and/or those from culturally, linguistically diverse, and economically poor backgrounds, significant work remains. This is particularly true in urban settings which overwhelmingly serve students who are economically poor, culturally and linguistically diverse and lag significantly behind their peers in academic achievement. For example, more than ever schools are enforcing stricter discipline policies (e.g. zero tolerance) which in turn have contributed to the delinquency of minority youth, especially Latino and African American youth, and increased rates of minority incarceration Minority youth comprise over 60 percent of children detained by juvenile justice systems across the United States (Esposito & Normore, in press). These students are more than eight times as likely as their white peers to be housed in juvenile detention facilities. In all but a few cases, these juveniles passed through traditional educational organizations on their way to incarceration. This path is commonly referred to as the *school to prison pipeline* and represents a failure of our educational institutions, and our communities, to serve all students in their care. Truly a moral and ethical imperative, rooted within a social justice framework, exists to ameliorate such failures.

The achievement of all students must be viewed both as an economic and moral imperative. The majority of the extant educational literature uses the term *Inclusion* to reference the practice of educating students with *identified* disabilities in the general education setting. This concept stems from the United States 2004 amended *Individuals with Disabilities Education Improvement Act,* and its subsequent amendments, which mandate that students with disabilities be educated in the general education setting to the maximum extent possible. The emphasis within the existing special education literature on the legal mandates of IDEIA underscores the fact that individuals with disabilities have faced and continue to face discrimination within schools and society. However, inclusion as we know it today is rooted in a philosophy that emphasizes the uniqueness of all learners, not just students with disabilities. An emphasis on high quality classrooms and schools—that are welcoming and affirming to all students, especially those most at risk for failure is both a moral and ethical obligation for society and school systems alike.

In the book *The Prison Path: School Practices that Hurt Our Youth* Christen Clemson breaks from the compliance of tranquil minds, courageously examining issues that deal with a plethora of challenges to our educational system and its relation to the prison systems in the United States. Clemson pushes us to tackle issues found in both schools and prisons, their impact on both institutions, and how they feed each other. She helps us: trace the religious history of schools and how schools are used to instill values, morality, testing, sorting, labeling and punishing; how the history of the prison system evolved, and brings us to an understanding of how the system currently exists within the social system by identifying the types of people who are incarcerated, the power held by the institution, and its shared institutional mission with schools to educate; the power and moral dimension of institutions and how institutions designate good or bad through the social lessons it teaches through where they are built and how they label; how the labeling process for diagnosing students with special needs mirrors the labeling and sorting process for inmate classification and prison assignment; the importance of space in each institution and how space given to students versus space of inmates, where each institution is located, how entry to each institution is gained, and the barriers; prison gangs and high school cliques, the roles that social groups and peer norms play in schools compared to the social groups and gangs in prison, why people join, what power they have, types, and how to deal with them; details the scandals that have arisen, why ethics in each institution is so hard to maintain, and starting from the ground up (little kids) to make ethical leaders; private prisons and charter schools - the similarities in missions, funding, and the idea of each institution as a commodity; school discipline and the juvenile justice system - similarities in how each work, how they feed into each other, a discussion on School Resource Officers and their role in schools and the juvenile justice system. Clemson challenges us to consider the changes we need to make, personal examination of how we teach, learn, how we teach teachers, focus on our students strengths, teacher strengths, ask to ourselves difficult questions about why we teach.

According to the United States Department of Justice's Office of Juvenile Justice and Dequincy Prevention, the juvenile arrest rate for all offenses in the United States reached its highest level in the 1990s, and then declined 43 percent by 2010. In 2010, there were 4,857 arrests for every 100,000 youths ages 10 through 17 in the United States (U. S. Dept. of Justice, 2012). However, when collecting juvenile arrest rates for all crimes in the nation by race, the US department of Justice fails to disaggregate the data for Latinos. The Office of Juvenile Justice and Delinquency Prevention justifies this failure to identify juvenile arrest rates for Latinos by concluding persons of "Hispanic" ethnicity may be of any race, i.e., white, black, American Indian, or Asian. (U. S. Department of Justice, 2012). The structural crisis of the capitalist system as a whole only exacerbates the challenges articulated and analyzed so meticulously in Clemson's important volume by an author uniquely adept and positioned in exposing the exploitative privileges at work in institutions. Education's social and metabolic control over the lives of our youth reflects the policies and practices of the capitalist elite who target the most vulnerable populations in the poorest countries by means of austerity programs. We need a sustainable ecology of educational practices that sustains solutions to the crisis of public education today, policies and practices that refuse to squander the lives of our most marginalized youth who often end up incarcerated. Study after study indicates that prevention and treatment programs are more effective than incarceration, and that it is cheaper and more effective to keep less serious juvenile offenders in the community, where they can access needed services and avoid or limit disruption in their home lives. The evidence also shows that it is ineffective to lump delinquent kids together in large institutions far from home. The challenge then remains in reforming the juvenile justice system, which takes a shifting of resources, and political will.

Study after study into youth residing in the juvenile justice system reveals some of the realities they face. The most serious youth offenders enter the juvenile justice system with histories that include depression, physical and sexual abuse, witnessing violent acts, parental substance abuse and neglect, and numerous mental health, developmental, and emotional issues. The extensive amount of trauma found in incarcerated youth must be identified, taken into consideration, and provided treatment. If the expectation for the youth exiting the juvenile justice system is not to reoffend, the juvenile justice system must provide the services and attention necessary while they are incarcerated. For youth residing in our juvenile justice systems getting access to treatment and staying in treatment is a real challenge. One of the ways to provide treatment, and treatment retention, is for our juvenile system and courts to make treatment a priority over incarceration. Some of the most promising interventions for incarcerated adolescents of any ethnicity include outpatient family-based interventions, problem solving, social skills training, and school-based recovery programs. Until this decade, recovery programs on school campuses, and stand-alone recovery schools existed mostly in isolation. Like the juvenile courts, these recovery programs and schools operate with unique requirements and treatment options with the purpose of advocating, promoting, and strengthening recovery programs and schools (Marietti, Tucker and Normore, in press).

Another issue critical to this discussion is prison education programs for adults. Available research in the area of correctional education and prison-based education (Karpowitz & Kenner, 2004) takes a penetrating look at the needs and challenges of society's disenfranchised - the denizens of our streets, the emotionally and physically incarcerated, our children in juvenile hall and in unsettled homes. Correctional institutions have operated as warehouses for too long, simply locking up offenders without any real effort to rehabilitate or educate. The results have been unacceptably high rates of recidivism throughout the nation, with a national average of more than 68 percent (Baca, 2010). This means that for every ten people released from custody, seven individuals will be rearrested, reconvicted, and resentenced for a new crime within three years. It is incumbent to encourage public awareness of the causes that underlie the destructive cycles plaguing these populations, including the abuse and neglect that cycle through generations. Changing the ways correctional institutions operate requires us to think differently about the purpose, structures, and values of the current system. *The Prison Path: School Practices that Hurt Our Youth* is a book whose author evidently is exceptionally gifted for her success in refusing to let the voices of dissent remain marginalized in our discussion of education in the twenty-first century. Clemson has done this by tackling issues found in both schools and prisons, their impact on both institutions, and how they feed each other. Further, she presents ideas for how to change or modify them and refuses to disregard the context of the external world when planning and plotting prison and educational reform. The upshot of her work compels us to examine not only how educational policies are produced for the least advantaged in our schools, but how educators and students are themselves produced in the wider institutional, cultural and economic arrangements of US society. It is a book that will prove invaluable to all who choose to call themselves educators. The book is crafted from the professional experiences, intellectual engagements, and moral commitments of the author. It is based on foundation of equal and social justice concerning a multitude of lenses used to view and attempt to understand the factors that contribute to the pathway to prison, the relationship between crime and education, and the need for those with a vested interested in programs and support structures that promote and foster collaboration of those who lead and work in education, social work, mental health facilities, law enforcement agencies, and correctional facilities

Recognition that the role of leaders in any organization is at least in part to advocate on behalf of traditionally marginalized and poorly-served citizens carries a corollary contention that traditional hierarchies and power structures must be deconstructed and reconfigured, thereby creating a new paradigm that subverts a longstanding system that has privileged certain citizens while oppressing or neglecting others. This would mean that organization leaders must increase their awareness of various explicit and implicit forms of oppression. They need to develop an intent to subvert the dominant paradigm, and finally act as a committed advocate for educational change that makes a meaningful and positive change in the education and lives of traditionally marginalized and oppressed students and extend their scope of influence well beyond the walls of their institutions. Given this perspective, educators are potentially the architects and builders of a new social order wherein traditionally disadvantaged peoples have the same educational opportunities, and by extension social opportunities, as traditionally advantaged peoples (Giroux, 1998) in order to curb the school to prison pipeline.

REFERENCES

Baca, L.D. (2010, March/April). Education based incarceration: Changing the way weincarcerate. *Sheriff Magazine, 62*(1), pp. 54–58.

Choate, B., & Normore, A.H. (2013). Leadership's role in reducing jail violence and
recidivism. In Normore, A.H., & Erbe, N. (Eds.), *Collective efficacy as a multidisciplinary approach to leadership development: International perspectives* (pp. 163-182). Bingley, UK: Emerald Group Publishing Limited.

Esposito, M.C., & Normore, A.H. (in press, 2015). *Inclusive practices and social justice*
leadership for special populations in urban settings: A moral imperative. Chapel Hill, North Carolina. Information Age Publishing.

Giroux, H. A. (1998). *Channel surfing: racism, the media, and the destruction of today's youth.* New York: St. Martin's Press.

Karpowitz, D., & Kenner, M. (2004). *Education as crime prevention: The case for*
reinstating Pell grant eligibility for incarceration. Annandale-on-Hudson, NY: Bard College.

Marietti, P., Tucker, J., & Normore, A.H. (in press, 2015). Chemically dependent
adolescent Latino offenders: restorative and social justice as alternatives to incarceration. In K. Esposito and A.H. Normore (Eds.), *Inclusive practices and social justice leadership for special populations in urban settings: A moral imperative* (pp. xxx–xxx). Chapel Hill, North Carolina. Information Age Publishing.

U. S. Department of Justice (2012, December 17). *Office of Juvenile Justice and*
Delinquency Prevention. Retrieved from OJJDP Statistical Briefing Book: http://ojjdp.gov/ojjstatbb/crime/JAR_Display.asp?ID=qa05200.

ONE

Why We Do What We Do

Formal[1] schooling and education have played a huge role in shaping the United States. Education's early roots were firmly entrenched with religion to promote the spread of education to combat the fear of Satan. As education in the United States has progressed, it has been used to convert, instill morality, educate, stratify, control, capitalize upon, test, label, organize, and punish the children who attend. This brief overview of education in the United States touches on all of these moments and then explains how these factors affect schools and prisons today.

Education existed in the Americas long before Christopher Columbus landed on the shores of the New World. Most of the Native American tribes that lived in the New World had an education system that involved adults fostering a sense of independence for children in their collectivistic society where people relied on one another, encouraging one another's strengths and supporting their differences. For example, if one child was blind, the other children adapted their own behavior as they recognized the blind child's excellent hearing skills in comparison with their own. In this way, there were no weaknesses, and everyone had a strength to be admired. Learning was an ongoing event that was not limited to a specific time or space. With the arrival of the Pilgrims, education in the New World changed dramatically.

Formal education arrived with the Puritans as they settled on the Massachusetts shore in the 1630s.[2] Puritans were Protestants who chose to come to the New World to avoid the persecution they faced in England. The Protestantism that the Puritans brought to the New World stripped away the fabricated rules of English Protestantism and lived by the direct word of the Bible. Puritans came to the New World seeking a place to live and worship with a freedom that was not given to them in England. They wished to establish new communities based on their relig-

1

ious preferences; to accomplish this, Puritans believed that everyone had to be able to read the Bible. Teaching young children to read the Bible became a crucial part of the success of the religion.

Since the Puritans preached that all were born in sin and the only way to reach heaven was through repentance, life was a constant struggle between good and evil. The fear of Satan and eternal damnation made learning morality a crucial part of a Puritan child's education. Free schooling was offered to all Puritan children and the first Puritan school, Roxbury Latin School, was opened in 1635.[3] Roxbury Latin School was a small school that focused on teaching its students how to become good citizens through a classical education in Latin, special courses in moral education, and religious training.[4] While the Roxbury Latin School mainly educated young boys, Dame schools existed in the kitchen or living room of a teacher's home where reading and writing were taught to both boys and girls.[5] In 1639, Harvard College was established in Cambridge, Massachusetts, so that Puritan boys could continue their education and become ministers and community leaders.[6]

The majority of children in New England attended reading-and-writing schools, "which provided an authoritarian education and taught only the skills necessary to read and understand religious and civil decrees."[7] Once they left the reading-and-writing school, boys were faced with three options: attend a Latin school to further enhance their education, train with their father, or take an apprenticeship with a craftsman.[8] Attendance at a Latin school meant furthering a classical education, and college was reserved for those who desired to be ministers or public leaders.[9] Most boys trained in the crafts of their father, since apprenticing with a craftsman required that the family of the apprentice pay room and board, which was a great expense for the family. Apprenticeships lasted for approximately seven years; once completed, a young man could open his own shop or take over from his father or teacher.[10]

As Puritan communities expanded, leaders believed that the religious teachings by parents and masters were lacking. In 1642, a law was passed that required parents and masters to teach children under their care the principles of religion and the laws of the commonwealth.[11] This was one of the first laws to set a minimum competency in reading and writing. Five years later, the Old Deluder Satan Act was passed since many believed that the 1642 law was not being implemented. The 1647 law required towns of fifty or more families to hire a schoolmaster to teach reading and writing.[12] For towns with one hundred or more families, a grammar school master needed to be hired to prepare children for further education.[13]

By 1700, there were thirty-nine grammar schools in the New England area.[14] Books for these schools were made by the city of Boston, which was the second largest printing center in the New World.[15] Puritans took advantage of the popularity of the printing press and printed books on morality for their children to use. In the North, schools became as important as churches for putting children on the path to salvation and God. With Protestantism firmly entrenched in the North, Lutherans, Calvinists, and Catholics in the middle region, and Anglicans in the South, religion dominated the New World.

Throughout the 1700s and into the early 1880s, religion dominated the schools in the North. The South, however, was a different matter entirely. Southerners believed that education was a private matter, to be handled within their own homes. Distance also played a factor; whereas towns in the North were close together, the plantation system in the South meant that wide distances separated homes. Creating a central space for a school was nearly impossible. The Anglican Church, which dominated religion in the South, did not value education as a way to further religious beliefs. Therefore, wealthy plantation owners were free to hire private tutors to educate their children.

The Revolutionary War interrupted the lives and education of many new Americans as they fought for freedom from Britain. As the newly formed United States began to rebuild after the war, the North became an industrial hub. Manufacturing and cottage industries appeared in the North as Northerners drew on their religious upbringing and touted learning as a way to achieve happiness. In the South, agriculture ruled the land. Once plantations owners' sons returned home, they learned to manage their plantations by apprenticing with their fathers. As debates took place in Philadelphia to shape the future of America, education played a prime role in those discussions.

Churches, especially churches in the North, wanted to control the schools in the new nation. Protestantism viewed schools as a way to educate youth in the gospel and beliefs of the church. Framers of the Constitution worried that allowing churches to control the education of the new nation would create a problem; the answer lay in the Bill of Rights, which granted the control of schools to state governments in 1791.

Schools taught moral and religious values, as well as virtue, patriotism, courage, hard work, and social order. It was not until the 1820s that teaching tools like globes, maps, and chalkboards appeared.[16] Schools in Northern cities started implementing uniforms, age-graded classrooms, superintendents (nonteaching teachers), textbooks, and high schools.[17] City schools became acknowledged centers of learning as they built huge schools, complete with Roman and Greek columns to give schools a hallowed air, in cities that reeked of smoke, dirt, and sewage. Even though these buildings attempted an air of enlightenment on the outside, inside they were little better than the cities themselves. Crowded, small, dimly lit classrooms with poor ventilation, flights upon flights of steps, poor building scheduling, and countless other inconveniences made teachers' jobs a nightmare.[18]

Teachers suffered from a range of diseases, some life threatening, often caught from students or from poor working conditions.[19] Due to the chaotic scheduling of students and new attempts at pedagogy, teachers often found themselves making numerous trips up and down narrow flights of stairs, spending time in drafty, damp, and cold rooms, or suffering in scorching hot classrooms that lacked windows.[20] Students endured the same conditions and problems as teachers, often finding cutting class a more pleasant experience than coming to school. Teachers attempted to implement the principles they had learned in normal school—control, order, discipline, and teaching strategies—but most were barely older than their students and struggled to maintain control.[21]

Schools in the early 1800s were primarily for teaching morals, but some schools were starting to teach secular subjects like literacy, numeracy, and basic knowledge. In 1821, the high school was developed from privately funded academies.[22] These high schools were a place where students were taught useful skills and common knowledge, instead of the classic Latin education. By 1830 in the North, more people wanted tax-supported, free schools to educate the masses.[23] With thousands of immigrants entering the Northern port cities, schools began to be tasked with the chore of teaching English, basic knowledge, and morals to the arriving immigrant children.

In these Northern cities, school numbers began to increase dramatically as opportunities for apprenticeships declined and skilled laborers were replaced with machines.[24] Schools in cities had age-graded classrooms and standardized curriculum and teaching pedagogies. Reformers believed that "in an ideal school, children of roughly the same age proceeded through school together, read the same books, and encountered more difficult material as they climbed the academic ladder."[25]

The few schools that had appeared in the South were in major cities and served as places for orphans or homeless children. These schools were similar to boarding schools and offered students the very basics in education. Private tutors continued to be the preferred educational methods of prosperous plantation owners. In the 1830s, the South made it a crime to educate a slave or an African American. Education in the South was viewed as a Northern phenomenon, with the South refusing to build schools, require mandatory attendance, or establish teachers' colleges.

Most students were educated using two of the most well known books, *McGuffey's Reader* and the *New England Primer*. *McGuffey's Reader* was written by Reverend William Holmes McGuffey and used the Bible to help teach moral and religious lessons, patriotism, hard work, courage, virtue, and honesty.[26] *McGuffey's Reader* outsold all other books, except the Bible, and became the unofficial curriculum of most schools since copies passed from generation to generation.[27]

Immigration once again became a major issue. From 1830 to 1850, approximately one million Catholics moved to the Northern cities in search of work and cheap housing.[28] Protestants shunned these new arrivals, limiting their access to schools and jobs. In areas where Catholics were allowed to attend school, Catholics requested that schools use Catholic prayers and the Catholic Bible to teach their children. Catholics believed, like Protestants, that if their children were not taught using the Catholic Bible and ideologies, then the mission of the church would fail.[29] When Protestants refused to allow the Catholic Bible and ideologies into their schools, Catholics sought to create their own schools. Protestant leaders who controlled the distribution of wealth refused to relinquish the money and violent protests arose. These aggressive encounters and push for Catholic schooling began the parochial school movement in the United States.

Between 1852 and 1918 mandatory attendance laws went into effect in all states. These new laws, combined with laws that made it illegal to employ children in factories, sent school attendance skyrocketing. Children entered schools that now ran in an orderly fashion; every day started with a prayer, a Bible reading, and the Pledge of Allegiance or a patriotic song.[30] A bell rang and lessons began; another bell rang and the lesson ended; rules were stringently enforced and punctuality was akin to religion.[31] The bell system managed so much more than time; a supporter of the system described a "Timepiece, of some kind, in every schoolroom, so placed that all the children can see it. It relieves their bodies by its assurance that the time for relaxation is approaching; and it stimulates their minds by its admonition, that the sands of time are wasting."[32] Clocks, bells, and schedules had now become a focus of education.

During this time, the American Civil War broke out. Between the years of 1861 and 1865, the North and the South engaged in a bloody battle over slavery. When the North emerged victorious in 1865, Northerners went to the South hoping to help them rebuild and reintegrate Southern society. During Reconstruction, Northerners who were appalled by the lack of free and public education brought mass education to the South. African-Americans and former slaves sent their children to school, hoping to combat the 95 percent illiteracy rate; students entered school hoping for literacy and a classical education.[33]

White reformers felt that educating African-Americans and former slaves with a classical education was not feasible or appropriate; Whites argued that African-Americans should receive a vocational education. Some Southerners advocated for schools for African-Americans; they argued that schools taught responsibility, self-help, morality, respect, and law and order.[34] When the North withdrew in 1877, African-American schools were closed and Jim Crow laws were passed with zeal. In the 1896 Supreme Court decision *Plessy v. Ferguson,* the Court ruled that separate accommodation on railways cars was legal, so long as the accommodations were equal. This ruling spawned everything from separate bathrooms and drinking fountains to schools and churches.

While Northerners bemoaned the changes in the South, the North was far from an ideal place for African-Americans and minorities. Minorities and African-Americans lived in urban ghettos in crowded cities where they received inadequate health care, and were subject to job discrimination and segregated schooling opportunities that barely taught rudimentary skills.[35] School critics complained that schools had not fixed the social order, improved poverty, or enhanced culture.

Meanwhile, the West was battling both religion and race. Catholicism was prevalent in the West because of the Spanish influence. As settlers moved West, Protestantism and Anglicanism spread. Spanish-speaking schools that had existed for years stopped being recognized in the 1890s when White settlers began to claim land.[36] Spanish speaking people in the West began to be treated like African-Americans in the South; their schools were closed, their religion shunned, and their language forbidden. Whites sent students who spoke limited or no English to Mexican Preparatory schools where they could learn English and basic skills.[37]

Around the turn of the century, pedagogy took center stage. One new method, "object" teaching, was introduced by John Pestalozzi, a Swiss education reformer, and emphasized the importance of using everyday objects in the learning process. Pestalozzi reformers helped to make schools more child-centered, a place where children drove their own learning and learned to love learning. In reality, however, most teachers found these methods difficult to include in their schools, so they relied on trusted methods like rote memorization, recitation, and drills.

Hiram Orcutt, a contemporary of Pestalozzi's, advocated a mechanized approach to education. Orcutt believed, "Every arrangement in the school should be systematic. There should be a time for everything, and everything in time; a time to open the school, which should never vary; a definite time for every school exercise; a time for study and a time for recess; a time to whisper and a time to keep silent."[38] He believed that children thrived in a strict and orderly environment. Many teachers in Northern city schools agreed with Orcutt's principles because they helped to maintain control within these busy and chaotic city schools. Orcutt's model seemed to fit the changing landscape; elementary and high school enrollments in the 1900s went from 15.5 million to 25.7 million.[39]

These numbers were bolstered by the influx of immigrants coming from central and southern Europe; between 1890 and 1918, 18.2 million immigrants arrived.[40] Americans worried that these new immigrants would destroy the nation. Ellwood P. Cubberley wrote that the new immigrants were idiotic, unmotivated, illiterate, lazy, and did not understand order.[41] Schools were called on to fix these defects by creating a fixed social order, better skills, literacy, motivation, and respect.[42]

Women rallied to this call for improved schools, reforming schools by adding gardens, playgrounds, and home economics classes; supplying lunches to the poor; adding libraries; and instituting a multitude of other reforms. John Dewey was considered the "father of progressive education" and his ideas became the rallying point for many of these women. Dewey believed that schools should be used as institutions through which social reforms were taught and children should be active participants in learning how to live in a democratic society.[43] This learning should be achieved using hands-on experiences or, as Dewey called it, "experiential learning," which provided context and frameworks that allowed children to learn through action and reflection.[44]

Dewey's main educational reform rival was Ellwood P. Cubberley, who believed that education should be run with efficiency, organization, and discipline. Cubberley promoted the business model, in which particular groups perform specific and specialized jobs overseen by a chain-of-command administration and a centralized authority. Cubberley believed this system would help maximize the productivity of schools, especially in the areas of educational administration. Cubberley "emphasized that the schools are, in a sense, factories in which the raw products (children) are to be shaped and fashioned into products to meet the various demands of life."[45]

Social efficiency became the mode by which schools would be run: "schoolrooms and buildings were standardized, school leadership became autocratic (imitating military oligarchies), and teachers were often subordinates expected to 'carry out the dictates of administrators, supervisors, and courses of study.'"[46] No longer would the system adjust to meet the needs of the individual child; rather, the child must fit himself or herself into the system or be left behind. School advocates who had once believed that schools were the great equalizer in society now felt that nothing could be done to help individuals who lacked either ability or achievement; education magnified the difference between individuals instead of eliminating it.[47]

This emphasis on mechanization in school was reinforced by the excitement for standardized testing that came with World War I. Between the early 1910s and the 1930s, hundreds of standardized tests appeared; most came from the military's attempt to place men in the positions that suited their talents and education. These tests made their way to education, where students received intelligence testing, aptitude testing, vocational testing, and a wide variety of assorted tests. With as many as forty to fifty students in a classroom, many teachers used the test results to group students together based on their test scores. This became a type of ability grouping.[48] These tests were believed to be the panacea for social ills by allowing people to be sorted into the positions for which they showed the most aptitude.

The testing phase was temporarily pushed aside by the *Brown v. Board of Education* decision in 1954. While the *Plessy* decision had legalized the separate but equal idea, the *Brown* case overturned that decision within educational facilities. De jure segregation, or the deliberate segregating of races in schools, was no longer allowed, and schools were ordered to comply with desegregation with haste.[49] Schools in the North proceeded with this decree slowly, but Southern schools refused violently. Prince Edward County in Virginia closed every public school in the county and opened private, Whites-only schools until this practice was ruled illegal in 1964.[50] Other areas in the South ignored or disobeyed the desegregation ruling until the 1960s.

The Soviet launch of the satellite Sputnik into orbit in 1957 eclipsed race issues. The Soviets had beaten America into space, a major triumph during the Cold War. America panicked, blaming schools for not preparing students to compete academically on an international level. The National Defense Education Act (NDEA) was signed into law in 1958 and authorized the use of federal funding for schools. In 1960, $20 million was spent on teaching aids like the Vistitutor. These aids were supposed to remove the subjectivity from teaching, improving the learning of all students. Aids like the Vistitutor never lived up to their expectations and teachers once again became the center of the classroom.

The focus on education did not diminish, however. In the mid to late twentieth century, an increased federal focus on education came about with the passing of NDEA (1958), the Elementary and Secondary Education Act (ESEA; 1965), Back to Basics (1975), 1982's pressure for direct instruction, and 1983's *Nation at Risk*. The ESEA in 1965 was the first piece of legislation that provided funding for schools with disproportionate numbers of poor students and funded programs like Head Start. One of the biggest challenges facing schools in the 1960s was how to educate middle- and lower-class children together.[51] During this time, the Civil Rights movement was cresting. In the South, courts ordered schools to bus poor, mostly African-American students from their home schools to White, wealthy schools, creating forced diversity.[52] Schools suffered the brunt of this turmoil with situations like the Little Rock Nine being splashed across televisions and radios.

The Civil Rights movement extended to people with disabilities as well. In 1975, President Ford signed legislation that mandated that children with disabilities be placed in the least restrictive environments possible. This came after the nation saw a 142 percent increase in students being labeled "disabled."[53] Minority boys were labeled disabled at a much higher rate than White boys, which added to the tensions between communities and schools. White flight, an oil embargo, and skepticism of the government increased the conflict. Polls showed that society believed schools were in trouble and needed to focus more on basics, enforce discipline policies, and set higher standards for their students.[54]

The focus in education during 1973 turned to the unequal funding of schools. In 1973, the Supreme Court ruled that there was not a constitutional right to equally funded schools.[55] This meant that inner-city schools were faced with declining tax bases as Whites left the city to go to the more affluent suburbs. Support for this legislation came from stagnant National Assessment of Educational Progress scores. States believed that passing minimum competency exams would help, so in 1980 many states passed legislation that supported more testing. *Nation at Risk*, a report published in 1983 on the state of American schools, threw the nation into panic. The report said that America was facing a generation of students who were illiterate in science and mathematics and placed far behind students in Japan and China on tests like the Scholastic Achievement Test and the American College Test. Critics complained loudly that American education lacked uniform standards across the country.

These critics believed that competition might help public school districts improve. In 1985, legislation was passed that paved the way for charter schools, many of which were run by chief financial officers and other former business managers. Education was now viewed as a tangible good that could be produced and purchased by choosing the right school to attend. Even cities attempted to use charter schools in place of their failing schools; Philadelphia was one of the first cities to use charter schools as a "school-within-a-school" concept.[56]

The early 1990s saw the first self-proclaimed "education president" elected. President George H. W. Bush ran on a plan called America 2000, which called for national standards, standardized testing nationally, and the involvement of businesses, technology, labor, and researchers in developing a curriculum for schools.[57] President Bush Senior advocated for charter schools as a viable option to improve American education, and by 1995 nineteen states had passed legislation allowing charter schools. Following President Bush's four years in office, President Bill Clinton was elected to office in 1994.

President Clinton built on America 2000, which he renamed the Educate America Act: Goals 2000. President Clinton called for two new goals: increased parental involvement and better teacher development.[58] Goals 2000 was an attempt to make sure that all students would be literate and leaders in mathematics and science, and that graduation rates would rise.[59] To ensure that the goals were met, testing was required in grades three through eight, and schools with consistently low or bad performance marks would be penalized. Goals 2000 marked the first time that the federal government looked to punish schools that underperformed.

President Clinton's Goals 2000 was followed in 2002 by President George W. Bush's No Child Left Behind Act (NCLB). NCLB's goal was to use testing and accountability to eliminate differences in school performance based on race, ethnicity, and socioeconomic status.[60] Schools that could not meet the adequate yearly progress (AYP) goals were threatened with financial cuts. Educators bemoaned the required yearly testing that came with NCLB and many worried that meeting all of the goals of the new mandate would be impossible. NCLB set goals for attendance rates, graduation rates, dropout rates, and passing percentages; this meant that schools could be punished for failing to meet one or all of the requirements.

Despite the worries of educators, researchers, and parents, NCLB was reauthorized again in 2007 with stricter punishments for schools that failed to meet AYP. Many poor, struggling schools pushed their worst students into special education classes,[61] encouraged them to be absent on testing days, or forced students to drop out. Numerous scandals arose in schools as these detrimental practices were exposed. One unexpected consequence of NCLB occurred when some states actually lowered their minimum requirements so that they would not face penalties.

With approximately fourteen thousand school districts in the United States responsible for fifty million students, the United States has the largest decentralized school system in the world.[62] Attending these schools are children of all ethnicities, genders, and races, with varying socioeconomic statuses, fluctuating levels of English fluency, and different educational needs. This means that schools are tasked with providing an education that meets the needs of all the students, the demands of the communities, and the requirement of state and federal laws. This is a daunting task for any school district; however, funding plays a huge role in how well a school can accomplish these goals. With the majority of school funding coming from local sources, poor schools are at a distinct disadvantage.

This disadvantage has been magnified by the turn in economics and jobs. At one time, high school dropouts had the ability to enter the workforce doing manual labor, in manufacturing jobs, or joining the military; today, however, few jobs are available to those without a high school diploma or even a college degree. That test scores of "poor and minority children remain relatively low is not particularly surprising, given the collapse of urban infrastructure, rise of single-parent households and persistent poverty, and widespread faith of parents in equal educational opportunity for all and extra for their own."[63] This mentality, equal opportunity for all but more of their own, has created some of the most phenomenal school districts in the world, while leaving those with fewer resources struggling.

In his first term, President Obama introduced a new initiative called Race to the Top, which provided funding to states that used innovative, compelling, and comprehensive educational reforms. During his second term in office, the Common Core movement has gained momentum. The Common Core movement looks to establish clear and concise guidelines for students in kindergarten through twelfth grade, with a focus on developing critical thinking skills, problem-solving abilities, and analytic skills in the areas of mathematics and English.[64] Currently forty-four states have adopted the Common Core standards.[65] Many Common Core supporters hope that common standards across all fifty states and territories will create a more even and united educational system.

In the United States in 1930, 248,000 public schools existed. In 2011, that number had decreased to 98,817.[66] Approximately 50.1 million students entered public elementary or secondary high schools in the fall of 2013 and were taught by 3.3 million full-time teachers.[67] These numbers are large and hard to comprehend; however, they show the growth and evolution of the American education system. Many schools in the United States are now equipped with the latest in technology, bringing learning into the twenty-first century.

Even for schools that are not equipped with the latest technology and struggle to provide the best for their students, education is certainly different than it was in 1800s. No longer do students need to own their own materials and to pass the material down through the generations. Schools now provide health care, lunch, and even after-school programs to ensure that students have someplace safe to be while their parent or guardian is at work. In the current era, some schools have become an institution that provides a home-like atmosphere for students who need it. This is a far cry from the one-room school house, but education is not done changing or evolving.

In its long and storied history, education has been viewed as a salvation, the great equalizer, and as a sorting mechanism. Even today, education is viewed as the pathway to success for those who have had success with school and education. For those against whom education has waged war,[68] education can seem almost prison-like. Like John Dewey, most of society believes that education is still the fundamental path to improve society,[69] but what is the cost?

It is crucial that we ask ourselves this question: Is it possible that education limits more than it enhances? It seems that recent federal legislation has turned education into prison in its ability to test, label, organize, and punish those that do not match the definition of success. What message does this send to students? What happens to those students who are pushed or drop out? Can we say that receiving an education really opens doors when so few receive an education? How can we keep denying that money plays no role in the quality of a child's education, especially when the wealthiest in the country send their children to private schools? Even in 2014, education is expected to convert skeptics; teach right from wrong; provide learning; stratify socioeconomic groups; control the masses; capitalize on the success stories of the few; and test, label, organize, and punish those without resources, without capital, without connections, and without hope.

NOTES

1. Formal education here is defined by modern standards such as a school building, curriculum, and lesson materials.

2. *God in America: How Religious Liberty Shaped America,* directed by D. Belton (Motion Picture, 2010).

3. F. Washington Jarvis, *Schola Illustris: The Roxbury Latin School 1645–1995* (Boston: David R. Godine, 1995).

4. Ibid.

5. J. Spring, *The American School 1643–2004* (New York: McGraw-Hill, 2004).

6. Ibid.

7. Ibid.

8. K. Kizer, "Apprenticeship," retrieved June 15, 2004, from History of American Education Web Project: https://www3.nd.edu/~rbarger/www7/apprenti.html.

9. T. Miller, "Latin grammar schools," retrieved June 15, 2004, from History of American Education Web Project: https://www3.nd.edu/~rbarger/www7/latin-gra.html.

10. Ibid.

11. A. L. Matzat, "Massachusetts Education Laws of 1642 and 1647," retrieved June 15, 2004, from History of American Education Web Project: https://www3.nd.edu/~rbarger/www7/masslaws.html.

12. Spring, *The American School.*

13. Matzat, "Massachusetts Education Laws."

14. Spring, *The American School.*

15. K. Kizer, *Puritans,* retrieved June 15, 2004, from History of American Education Web Project: https://www3.nd.edu/~rbarger/www7/puritans.html.

16. Ibid.

17. Ibid.

18. K. Rousmaniere, *City Teachers: Teaching and School Reform in Historical Perspective* (New York: Teachers College Press, 1997).

19. Ibid.

20. Ibid.

21. Ibid.

22. Spring, *The American School.*

23. Reese, *America's Public Schools.*

24. Ibid.

25. Ibid.

26. Ibid.

27. Ibid.

28. J. Kern, "The Catholic Issue," retrieved June 15, 2004, from History of American Education Web Project: https://www3.nd.edu/~rbarger/www7/catholic.html

29. Ibid.

30. Reese, *America's Public Schools.*

31. Ibid.

32. Ibid.

33. Ibid.

34. Ibid.

35. Ibid.

36. Ibid.

37. Ibid.

38. H. Orcutt, *Hints to Common School Teachers, Parents, and Pupils; Or, Gleanings from School-Life Experience* (Boston, MA: Rutland GEO. A. Tuttle & Company, 1859, pg. 24).

39. Reese, *America's Public Schools.*

40. Ibid.

41. Cubberley as cited in Reese, *America's Public Schools.*

42. Reese, *America's Public Schools.*

43. J. Dewey, *Experience and education* (New York, NY: Simon & Schuster, 1938).

44. Dewey, *Experience and education.*

45. Cubberley as cited in Reese, *America's Public Schools.*

46. Reese, *America's Public Schools.*

47. Ibid.

48. Ibid.

49. *Brown v. Board of Education,* 347 U.S. 483 (United State Supreme Court May 17, 1954).

50. Reese, *America's Public Schools.*

51. Ibid.

52. Ibid.

53. Ibid.

54. Ibid.

55. J. Kozol, *Savage Inequalities: Children in America's Schools* (New York: Crown Publishers, 1991).

56. WestEd. "US Charter Schools," retrieved August 2000 from http://www.uscharterschools.org.

57. U.S. Department of Education: New York State Archives. *Federal Education Policy and the States, 1945–2009: The George H. W. Bush Years: America 2000 Proposed,* Retrieved from States' Impact on Federal Education Policy: http://www.archives.nysed.gov/ed-policy/research/res_essay_bush_ghw_amer2000.shtml.

58. H.R. 1804. *Goals 2000: Educate America Act,* Washington D.C., January 25, 1994, retrieved from http://www2.ed.gov/legislation/ GOALS2000/TheAct/index.html.

59. Reese, *America's Public Schools.*

60. Public Law 107-110 115 STAT. 1425. January 8, 2002, retrieved from U.S. Department of Education: http://www2.ed.gov/policy/elsec/leg/esea02/107-110.pdf.

61. Testing requirements are different for those in special education.

62. Reese, *America's Public Schools.*

63. Reese, *America's Public Schools.*

64. Common Core State Standards Initiative, retrieved 2014 from http://www.corestandards.org/.

65. Common Core State Standards Initiative.

66. National Center for Education Statistics, *Digest of Education Statistics, 2012* (NCES 2014-015), Chapter 2 (Washington, D.C.: U.S. Department of Education, 2013).

67. National Center for Educational Statistics, *Back to School Statistics,* Retrieved 2013 from http://nces.ed.gov/fastfacts/display.asp?id=372.

68. Native Americans, Catholics, European minorities, African-Americans, and Hispanics

69. Dewey, *Experience and education.*

TWO

Prison

The Historical Underpinnings

It might seem strange to devote an entire chapter to the history of prisons in a book that discusses the similarities between prisons and schools. The evolution of the prison has revolved around power; whoever has controlled the power has controlled the structure of punishment. From the beginnings of punishment in the form of tribal law, through the king as supreme power, and into a new democratic system, the punishments of choice have reflected the power shifts in society. The following pages contain a brief overview of prison history, followed by a brief exploration of how schools and prisons have shared similar institutional missions.

However, one of the first things that must be known is the current state of the prison system. Prisons face issues of overcrowding, maintaining security, and funding that are similar to issues faced by schools. Overall, the imprisonment rate for the United States is 480 prisoners per 100,000 residents, which currently leads the world.[1] In 2011, African-American inmates accounted for 38 percent of state inmates, White inmates accounted for 35 percent, and Hispanic inmates were at 21 percent.[2] As of October 26, 2013, the Bureau of Prisons held 211,195 federal inmates.[3]

In 2007, the national recidivism rate (i.e., number of people who return to prison on either a parole violation or a new charge) was 16 percent; however, this view is not complete.[4] Recidivism rates are tracked over the first three years of an inmate's release and the overall data is not promising. A ten-year study of eleven states conducted by the Bureau of Justice Statistics between 1983 and 1994 found that out of 108,580 released inmates, 63 percent were rearrested within three years.[5] Of those rearrested, 47 percent were arrested for a new crime and 41 percent returned to prison or jail.[6] In a larger study done in 1994 that encompassed fifteen states and 300,000 released inmates, 68 percent were arrested again within three years; of the 68 percent that were rearrested, 47 percent were convicted on a new crime.[7]

A study done by the Pennsylvania Department of Corrections found that the first year of release is the riskiest for inmates; most inmates violate parole and recidivate during this first year.[8] Young inmates face an increased risk of recidivism. An inmate younger than twenty-one when released is twice as likely to recidivate as an inmate who is older than fifty at the time of release.[9] Young inmates are especially problematic because they are often high school dropouts who have few skills and almost no training or education that qualifies them for legal employment.

In one form or another, punishment has existed for as long as there have been humans. However, the punishments historically looked much different than the punishments of today. Like education, discipline has evolved as people, societies, and life has changed. Some parts of this evolutionary process have been lost to time as many early codes of punishments were verbal or written. The one unique quality about codes of punishment was that they were built on prior codes; many had overlapping punishments for similar crimes.

One of the oldest codes of punishment was the Code of Hammurabi in Babylon, which lists approximately 282 laws. Of those 282 laws, twenty-five were punishable by death if violated.[10] Codes of punishment evolved and continued through the civilizations of Athens, Rome, and then to Britain. During the feudal era in Britain, codes of punishment were set and enforced by the lord of the manor. All who lived within the manor or town were owned by or answered to the lord of the manor. This meant that every manor or small town had its own set of rules and punishments. As the economic system in Britain began to move away from the barter and trade system and peasants realized their worth, manors began to collapse. The English split with the Catholic Church helped to finalize the end of the feudal system as the English king could now purchase knights instead of requiring the lords of the manor to supply knights. With the rise of the monetary system, the responsibility for creating and enforcing the rules came under the purview of the king.

Along with the king, the church and the family retained tremendous power in the realm of discipline. Family members who violated family rules faced stiff repercussions at home. Families were able to lock errant members away within their homes, punishing them as they saw fit, for the length of time they deemed suitable. Families worked hand in hand with the church, isolating family members who violated church policy. However, if a family was unable to detain a family member, or the church policy that had been violated was severe, the church could enforce their own punishments. Church punishments were often less severe than those issued by the courts, the king, or families.

A shift in power began around the 1600s as Britain became more unified under the power of the monarchy. Because the power was concentrated with the monarchy, anyone who performed a crime was considered to have committed the act against the king or queen. This direct violation of the monarch's will led to severe and swift punishment against the criminal. During this time the art of torture and executions reigned supreme. Hangings and tortures took place in the village squares, where the townsfolk gathered to watch the proceeding. At the beginning, these gatherings were mandatory and as time progressed, townsfolk made these proceedings a time of celebration. Officials believed that if they made a spectacle of the criminal, others would not be tempted to commit crime.[11] The monarch used these public scenes to display total and absolute power over the lives of his or her people.

As these executions became elaborate and performance-like, townsfolk gathered to watch for entertainment. Observers packed picnic lunches; criminals dressed in their most elaborate clothing and performed speeches, entertaining the crowds as they watched the executions. The invention of the guillotine in the 1790s helped to fuel this deathly show.[12] However, death was reserved for criminals who had committed the most severe crimes; there were no other options to punish the most egregious of crimes, since prison did not yet exist in their current form. Criminals who committed lesser crimes were punished through public humiliation, fines, imprisonment by family members, branding, or mutilation. The view of crime during this time was that it was an act committed against the monarch and an attempt to make the land lawless; therefore, it deserved swift and powerful retribution.[13]

As the types of crimes that were committed began to change, the power began to shift from the monarch to the victims of crime. The demand for skilled workers decreased and many people found themselves destitute, homeless, and resorting to crime. The English Parliament enacted laws that increased the number of homeless, vagrant, and pretty criminals.[14] As petty crime increased, the sentences for those crimes became harsher. Between the years of 1688 and 1815, the English penal code became known as "the Bloody Code" and the list of capital crimes rose from fifty to more than two hundred.[15]

Protests arose over the Bloody Code as the attitude toward the human body began to change. The purpose of the Bloody Code was to extract as much pain from the criminal as possible. Those who thought that this was cruel believed that punishment would be more effective if it punished the soul.[16] Along with this change in belief came a change in who issued punishments. Court became the entity that issued punishments to criminals; courts were able to sentence criminals with five different levels of severity.

The first level of severity was whipping, which was considered the least severe of all the punishments issued.[17] The second level of severity was burning or branding, depending on the crime committed.[18] Level three was mutilation, which meant notching ears, noses, or tongues and cutting off fingers or toes.[19] The fourth level of severity was a merciful and swift death, whereas level five was a tortured and slow death.[20] Those who received the extreme penalty, a tortured and slow death, were not allowed burial; their bodies were left out in a field near town to rot and serve as a lesson to those within the town.

Criminals such as debtors, vagrants, and the poor who committed lesser crimes faced public humiliation, fines, workhouses, hospitals, almshouses, penal transportation, and banishment.[21] As poverty became more prevalent in England and crime rates rose, the English began to rely on penal transportation as a way to combat crime. Petty criminals and chronic criminals were sent to the Americas and sold into indentured servitude.[22] During the pinnacle of the English penal transportation era, thousands of men, women, and children were sent to both America and Australia. After the Revolutionary War, English criminals were no longer wanted as indentured servants, so England was forced to send their criminals to Australian penal colonies. As penal transportation became unpopular in the late 1870s, England needed to find a new place to put their criminal populations.[23]

Ever resourceful, England turned their large decommissioned war and merchant ships into prison hulks. These leaky, drafty, barely floating old ships were turned into holding cells for criminals who could no longer be transported to America or Australia.[24] Many of these ships barely floated and inmates in lower decks often drowned as new holes opened up in the ships.[25] Whereas the large rooms used to hold debtors on land were dirty, smelly, and varmint- and bug-infested, hulks were even worse; most were wet and moldy; hot in summer and cold in winter; and home to malnutrition, illness, overcrowding, poor ventilation, and filth. Criminals sentenced to the hulks were forced to perform hard labor for the government or private contractors and consequently the life span for occupants of the hulks was short.[26]

Another type of punishment, the holding room, was reserved strictly for debtors. The debtors' prison was a large room holding debtors of all ages and genders.[27] Individual families ran many of these debtors' prisons and charged the debtors for food, clothing, and bedding.[28] This created a vicious cycle; debtors were in prison for lack of money and the additional charges for food, bedding, and clothes meant that these debtors stood almost no chance of ever paying off their debt or being free. Even though these rooms were crowded, dirty, smelly, and filled with rodents and disease, reformers believed that the answer to less brutal punishments began in these holding rooms.

Even though the idea of less severe punishments began in England, the United States eventually designed the first modern prison. To understand how the United States became the first to develop the modern prison, an understanding of how punishment developed in the United States is required. Like feudal England, the original thirteen colonies and their individual towns had rules and punishments that varied from town to town. As the signers of the Declaration of the Independence realized, if the Revolutionary War failed, they would receive the harshest punishments available under English law. This would mean a slow and tortured death back on English soil. With the memories of the Bloody Code still fresh in their minds, the new American citizens set about creating a new punishment code that protected society from the brutality of death.

To create this new set of punishments, Americans turned to the less gruesome English punishments as the basis for their new systems. While each town continued to have its own rules and punishments, many of these punishments focused on public humiliation and fines. Forms of public humiliation included the stocks, cages, or pillory, which displayed the criminal in the town center to be ridiculed by his neighbors. America still used the gallows, but death was a punishment reserved for the worst crimes committed by man.

Judges traveled on a routine circuit between small towns, hearing cases, and dispensing punishment. The jail, a large room with bars, often in the sheriff's house or a building within town, held the accused until the judge came back to town. Once the judge came back, the trial commenced, and if the accused was guilty, punishment was performed immediately.[29] Debt was the only crime for which long-term confinement was used. Debtors were locked away until their fine was paid, which meant that many were imprisoned for life or until their families could pay the debt.[30]

While the English Bloody Code punished more than two hundred crimes with death, Americans sought to simplify their penal code into four types of punishments: fines, public shame, physical chastisement, and death.[31] The most frequent punishment was fines; criminals were required to pay for the cost of the good or the damage, plus reparations, and then the criminal could go free. Since many thieves stole because they were poor, they could not pay the fine and were sentenced to debtors' prison. Public shaming, which ranged from the pillory to the wearing of a sign (e.g., the fictional Hester Prynne's scarlet letter A[32]) was used as a form of punishment. However, public shaming was only effective within small towns and by the 1700s, it had been replaced in most areas.

Physical chastisement took the place of public shaming; this included flogging, branding, notching, using torture devices, and mutilation; these punishments could be issued for slandering, gossiping, sedition, fortune telling, and drunkenness. For slanderers, gossips, or nags, gagging was often used, but when gagging was not enough, a heavy metal cage was placed over the head of the accused, and a spiked tongue of iron was inserted into the mouth so that the tongue rested on the spikes: this was called a "'gossip's bridle' or a 'scold's helm.'"[33] Whipping and flogging joined the pillory as a way to punish more severe incidents. Everything from treason and sedition to fortune telling and drunkenness could earn the criminal the pillory or the whip.

In 1771, William Carlisle of Rhode Island was convicted of passing counterfeit money; he received an hour in the pillory, cropping of both ears, and the letter R branded on both cheeks (for "rogue"), and the fine of $100.[34] Mr. Carlisle was fortunate; at the time, counterfeiting paper money carried a death sentence.[35] While not many crimes resulted in death, repeat criminals and criminals convicted of sexual deviance were put to death.

The final punishment during this time was death, which was adminis-tered through hanging. A person who was caught stealing a hog for the first time received a B for burglary brand on his right hand; caught a second time, a B was branded on his left hand, and on the third offense he was sentenced to death.[36] Crimes of sexual deviance resulted in death for a first offense. For example, a young boy of seventeen was convicted of committing buggery (having sexual relations) with a mare, a cow, two goats, five sheep, two calves, and a turkey; he was hanged immediately and the animals were punished by being executed and left to rot in a pit.[37]

As protests began to arise that punishments were becoming too grue-some and harkened back to the days of the English Bloody Code, reform-ers began to look for new ways to punish criminals. Many believed that the new punishment model should focus on changing the debtors' pris-on. The first prison model developed in the 1820s in Philadelphia, Penn-sylvania. This new prison model was based on the Quaker model of penance to God; inmates were sentenced to small amounts of time (thirty to forty months) and were taught a trade while locked away. Inmates were kept in individual cells consisting of a bed, a table, and chair; the roof of each room had a small skylight cut into it, so that as inmates prayed for forgiveness, the light of God could shine down upon them.

Silence was the key to the Pennsylvania system. Inmates never spoke and guards wore socks over their shoes to muffle the sounds. Each in-mate was placed in an individual cell that had its own recreational yard. Solid block walls separated prisoners, and doors were made of solid wood that did not allow prisoners to see out. Inmates were incarcerated so that they could examine their soul, find God, and when the time for release came, follow the law-abiding path of enlightenment.[38] In the Phil-adelphia model, inmates were treated humanely; the end goal was the reentry of the inmate into society as a productive citizen. A famous exam-ple of this type of prison is the Eastern State Penitentiary in Philadelphia, Pennsylvania.

Concurrently in 1816, the Auburn model developed in the Auburn Prison in New York. Unlike the Philadelphia model where the incarcera-tion was the punishment, the Auburn model used its inmates as penal slaves. Inmates were forced to work together in complete silence and faced harsh physical punishment if the rules were broken. The Auburn system created an alternate society within the prison where inmates were not kept caged like animals, but forced to work together to develop the skills they would need on their release.[39] The constant surveillance provided by the guards kept the inmates from acquiring bad habits or behaviors.[40]

The clock regulated inmate work inside the Auburn system. Inmates were assigned specific jobs within the prison to be done at precise times. When the bell rang within the prison, inmates were expected to have finished their assigned task and to move onto their next task. Guards observed each inmate or inmate work group and each was held accountable for his work and his time. Life within the Auburn system functioned on a grid-like structure; each moment of the day was linked to a specific task. Inmates were never idle; their work produced goods used by the prison and the excess was then sold to provide an income for the prison.

In selecting a prison model to implement throughout the United States, the Auburn system was chosen over the Philadelphia system for several reasons. Since inmates were put to work in the Auburn system, inmates mass produced goods that were then sold to support the prison. In the Philadelphia system goods were made, but on a much smaller scale and were often used by the inmate; therefore, the Philadelphia system was not self-supporting. Auburn prisons were cheaper to build and maintain since inmate labor was used in construction and in maintenance. These attributes helped to make the Auburn prison system the preeminent choice in prison systems for the United States.

In 1870, the American Prison Congress met to decide the future of the prison system.[41] Auburn-style prisons constructed around the country had become overcrowded and unsafe for both inmates and correctional officers. The Congress's decision resulted in the reformatory, which originally was built to house adult offenders. The first reformatory was built in Elmira, New York, in 1876 to house adult offenders, but it soon began to house youth offenders ages sixteen through thirty.[42] Elmira Reformatory was built on thirteen principles implemented in each reformatory. Between 1876 and 1913, seventeen states built reformatories and most were used to house youthful offenders.[43]

While new youth facilities were being built, adult facilities were undergoing changes. Between 1890 and 1930, new programs were implemented in adult facilities that gave inmates access to education, vocational training, family visits, libraries, and mail services. At the same time that inmates were being granted extra luxuries, more people were being incarcerated, which caused violence rates and security concerns to increase. With inmate populations increasing, the cost of housing inmates increased. Prisons began to create labor workshops, which mirrored factories, to produce goods at a faster rate. The government found that these new prison workshops could produce goods cheaply and gave many of their government contracts to prisons.

During World War I, these prison industries produced goods that aided the war effort cheaply and more efficiently than regular businesses. Labor unions and private businesses were outraged since prisons did not have to pay their workers and therefore could offer the goods at lower prices. In 1935, Congress passed the Ashurst-Sumners Act, which ended prison industries. However, the prison industry had brought about many changes in the prison system. Prisons now had programs for inmates, classified inmates according to violence level and mental abilities, and assigned inmates to specific jobs based on their abilities. [44]

Prison had become the place where inmates were confined and classified, and then the maximum in time and effort was extracted from them, resulting in the training of their bodies and the coding of their behavior; they were constantly visible to those in charge. [45] By the 1900s, the concept of the prison was so ingrained within society that it was hard to imagine a different type of punishment. Physical punishments had ceased to exist and prison had become the new justice that was supposed to be equal, autonomous, free from bias, and "the penalty of civilized societies." [46] With the advent of the prison, the penal system could now match the penalty with the crime. Criminals could now be sentenced to serve significant amounts of time since the prison now existed to hold them.

From the early 1900s until the 1940s, the U.S. inmate population increased by 147 percent and ten more Auburn-style prisons were built. [47] The focus of the prison up to this point had been teaching inmates skills that they could use upon their reentry into society. Sanford Bates, an attorney who later became Director of the Federal Bureau of Prisons, [48] believed that the answer to crime resided inside the individual; therefore, prisons needed to diagnose, find a cure, and then treat the inmate. [49] Bates referred to the inmate as a *patient* and argued that these patients needed treatment, which was administered inside the prison. On their release from treatment (prison), each patient needed a parole officer who would act as a therapist to continue the monitoring and treatment of the patient. [50]

According to Bates, since every patient was different, no one could know how long the treatment of a patient (inmate) would take. Therefore, the patient could not be sentenced to a specific amount of time; the determination would be made within the treatment center (prison). Bates's model ushered in the era of indeterminate sentences or sentences that provide a range of time (one to five years) instead of a specific amount of time. Patients who exhibited the hallmarks of the program, or the ability to internalize control within themselves, were considered ready for release. Internalized control focused on how a patient handled himself or herself in difficult situations within the prison, but unfortunately, control within the prisons would be severely tested as the Great Depression took hold.

With the passing of the Ashurst-Sumners Act in 1935, prison industrial complexes collapsed. This meant that prisons were no longer allowed to employ inmates in their factory-like settings. As the Great Depression lingered on and lawlessness increased, J. Edgar Hoover, the new director of the Federal Bureau of Investigation, began a war on crime. Hoover rejected research about the effects of prison on inmates and began to incarcerate criminals at high rates. This influx of new inmates combined with idle time and a large population of experienced inmates created a situation ripe for riots. Numerous prison riots occurred during this time, including a riot at Alcatraz in 1946.[51]

It took almost ten years for the prison system to regain control. By the 1960s, prisons had implemented new security systems and protocols. The Civil Rights Movement brought to light the way inmates had been treated and humane changes were made. A new belief about inmates also appeared, one that took into account the community and circumstances from which an inmate came.[52] The hope was that once the inmate was released, community resources would be used to help the inmate transition into the role of successful citizen. By putting into place plans like Head Start, poverty prevention programs, job training courses, and urban revitalization agendas, the new reintegration model attempted to change community factors that created the possibility for criminal behaviors.

The reintegration model was given a limited amount of time to work, because starting in the 1970s through the 1990s new get-tough laws gained favor with legislators and the public alike. These get-tough crime laws caused arrest rates to rise and incarcerations to skyrocket. Prisons, already crowded, now reached capacity and beyond. With the influx of new inmates came a change in sentencing. Instead of indeterminate sentences, judges began to issue sentences of a fixed amount of time and mandatorily pursuant to the crime committed. This led to the highest rates of incarceration in history; rates increased from 1 in every 218 people to 1 in every 142 people, and more than half were incarcerated for violent crimes.[53] In 2008, one in every one hundred people were incarcerated.[54]

This led to the record construction of prisons: "[B]etween 1998 and 1999 alone, the nation's corrections systems initiated the construction of 162 large new prison projects and launched 675 major renovations of existing facilities."[55] Many of these new prisons were designed to look like school campuses, complete with vocational centers, libraries, and churches.[56] Even with the massive building projects that took place in the late 1990s, get-tough laws filled these new prisons in a short time. With the massive overcrowding in prisons, the original ideals that prisons were built on have all but disappeared. These original ideals—to transform individuals' behavior, individualize penalties, assign work as a transformative element, and provide an education to all inmates—have been hard to accomplish because of the demands being placed on prisons.

Today, there are numerous types of prisons and they vary from federal to state and state to state. Most are roughly modeled off of the Auburn prison system model, where inmates are forced to work together. Within the modern prison system, there are seven basic types of prisons. The first type of prison is the minimum-security prison. These prisons have relatively low ratios of inmates to staff, dormitory housing, a barely defined boundary (meaning no razor wire) and are focused on work programs.[57] Facilities like these hold inmates that have committed nonviolent crimes and pose little danger to the community around them.

The second type of prison facility is the low-security facility. In low-security facilities, the inmate-to-staff ratio is slightly higher than the minimum-security facilities, the housing is mostly dormitory style, and there is often a double fence surrounding the perimeter of the facility; work and program pieces play a large role in low-security facilities.[58] Inmates housed here have either committed nonviolent crimes or proven themselves nonviolent enough to be granted permission to live in a low-security facility. In some instances, low-security prisons are next to minimum- or high-security facilities to combine costs.

The third facility type is medium security. In these facilities, the inmate-to-staff ratio is higher than the minimum- or low-security facility, the perimeters are strengthened with fence and wire, the housing is mostly cell-like, and there are more internal control measures.[59] Medium-security facilities have numerous work and program options, but these programs are housed within the facility itself. The majority of inmates within the United States are housed in prison facilities that are medium security.

High-security prisons have the strictest security features. These types of prisons are known as *penitentiaries* and exist on both the state and federal levels. Penitentiaries have highly secured perimeters that use fence, razor wire, and guard patrols, as well as the highest inmate-to-staff ratio, and have single or double inmate housing occupancy.[60] Inmate movement is highly controlled in a penitentiary setting.

Most people are more aware of these four types of facilities, but other types also exist. Juvenile facilities have appeared in greater numbers in the last twenty years. These facilities are designed to hold juveniles who have committed serious crimes or are deemed dangerous. Facilities that are designed for juveniles are slightly different than those designed for adults. There is an emphasis on providing classroom space, dormitory-style housing, and therapy rooms, which can provide the help that juveniles need.

At the federal and state levels, there are also administrative facilities. These facilities have designated special missions. For example, one administrative facility could be designated for holding pretrial inmates, another for inmates with serious and chronic medical problems, and yet another could house inmates who are escape prone. Administrative facilities can also include psychiatric facilities that incarcerate severely mentally ill inmates. These facilities have unique features designed by their selected designation.

The last type of prison facility is the military prison. Each branch of the Armed Forces has its own penal process as well as its own prison system. Most military prisons are for military personnel who have been found guilty or are awaiting trial on issues of national security. Military prisons have also been used to house prisoners of war. In recent years, controversy has surrounded the treatment of prisoners of war being held in U.S. military prisons.

No matter what type of prison an inmate is incarcerated in, for the majority, incarceration will not last forever. However, the odds of being incarcerated again are overwhelming. Three major studies have been done, two by the U.S. Department of Justice Bureau of Justice Statistics in 1999 and 2004 and one by the Pew Charitable Trust in collaboration with Associations of State Correctional Administrators, which gathered state-wide recidivism data and compiled it. The Pew researchers found that, when California is excluded (its sheer size skews the results), the average recidivism rate has been around 40 percent from 1994 through 2007.[61] (Excluding California from this compilation of data is problematic because California has the largest prison population in the United States.) This means that four out of every ten inmates who leave prison will likely return within three years.

Currently there are 216,265 inmates incarcerated in federal prisons. This number does not sound too unreasonable when compared with the 2012 population of the United States at 313.9 million.[62] However, when state prison populations are added into the totals, the number of those incarcerated increases. According to the website The Sentencing Project,[63] in 2012 approximately 2.2 million people were incarcerated in state or federal prisons. Incarcerating 2.2 million people is not cheap and according to a fact sheet put together by the National Association for the Advancement of Colored People approximately 70 billion dollars is spent on corrections each year.[64]

The consequences of incarceration are harsh; should an inmate regain his freedom, finding housing, obtaining gainful employment, staying sober, and adapting to life on the outside is difficult. Inmates are released with the clothing and possessions that they entered prison with and are sent back to their communities with instructions to check in with their parole officers. When these former inmates apply for jobs, housing, or public assistance, they must check the criminal history box and explain their past histories. Checking that box is almost a guarantee that the former inmate will be without a job, without housing, and without public assistance[65]; in fact, only 38 percent of ex-inmates are able to find employment.[66]

Prisons and schools have long shared missions that are eerily similar. Schools, with a mission to educate children, and prison, with a mission to reeducate those who have broken the norms and laws of society, share many similar traits. Throughout history, prisons have attempted to convert lawbreakers into law abiders, instill morality, educate, stratify, control, capitalize on, test, label, organize, and punish those who have broken the rules of society. Today our society uses prisons for punishment, control, and stratification. Society is perceived to be safer when drug dealers, thieves, and others are placed behind bars, safely out of sight and out of mind. However, at some point, most inmates will reenter society and their time in prison does little to help them reform or learn better habits.

In fact, a study by Donald T. Hutcherson shows that on average, spending time in prison helps inmates become better criminals and earn almost 11,000 dollars more per year illegally.[67] Hutcherson found that young former inmates who are gang members actually have the highest illegal earning potential, making prisons the criminal school. Within prison, young criminals are able to form connections and networks that lead to better criminal earnings.[68] Hutcherson argues, "You come in [to prison]. You're 16, 17, 18 years old. You're looking around and you're thinking 'Listen, I can learn from these seasoned veterans.' And that's exactly what you do."[69]

One of the startling facts about these young inmates is that almost 35 percent of people in 1996 had dropped out of school for behavioral issues, academic issues, or loss of interest in learning.[70] While they may lack traditional education, they are not stupid. Therefore, we must ask ourselves whether we want prisons teaching our young or do we want them taught in schools. If our answer is schools, then we must stop pushing students out or allowing them to drop out, because once they are gone from school, someone will give them an education. In today's world, they will most likely receive their new education in prison, becoming better, more talented criminals with every incarceration.

NOTES

1. K. McCarthy, "U.S. Prison Population Declined for Third Consecutive Year During 2012," Bureau of Justice Statistics, July 25, 2013, retrieved from http://www.bjs.gov/content/pub/press/p12acpr.cfm.

2. Ibid.

3. U.S. Department of Justice, Federal Bureau of Prisons, 2013, retrieved from http://www.bop.gov/about/statistics/population_statistics.jsp.

4. P. A. Langan and D. J. Levin, *Recidivism of Prisoners Released in 2004*, (Washington, D.C.: Bureau of Justice Statistics, 2002).

5. Ibid.

6. Ibid.

7. Ibid.

8. N. Bell, K. B. Bucklen, K. Nakamura, J. Tomkiel, A. Santore, L. Russell, and R. Orth, *Pennsylvania Department of Corrections: Recidivism Report 2013*, (Harrisburg, PA: Commonwealth of Pennsylvania: The Bureau of Planning Research and Statistics, 2013).

9. Ibid.

10. "Code of Hammurabi," *Legal History and Philosophy*, retrieved from http://www.commonlaw.com/Hammurabi.html.

11. M. Foucault, *Discipline and Punish: The Birth of the Prison* (Paris, France: Editions Gallimard, 1975).

12. "The History of the Guillotine," *The Guillotine Headquarters*, retrieved from http://www.guillotine.dk/pages/history.html.

13. Foucault, *Discipline and Punish*.

14. J. W. Roberts, *Reform and Retribution: An Illustrated History of American Prisons* (Baltimore, MD: United Book Press, 1997).

15. J. Lynch, "Cruel and Unusual: Prison and Prison Reform," *Colonial Williamsburg Journal*, 2011, retrieved from http://www.history.org/Foundation/journal/Summer11/prison.cfm.

16. Foucault, *Discipline and Punish*.

17. N. Morris and R. J. David, *The Oxford History of the Prison: The Practice of Punishment in Western Society* (Oxford, United Kingdom: Oxford University Press, 1998).

18. Ibid.

19. Ibid.

20. Ibid.

21. Ibid.

22. Roberts, *Reform and Retribution*.

23. Morris and David, *The Oxford History of the Prison*.

24. Roberts, *Reform and Retribution*.

25. Ibid.

26. Ibid.

27. Morris and David, *The Oxford History of the Prison*.

28. Ibid.

29. Lynch, "Cruel and Unusual."

30. Ibid.

31. Ibid.

32. N. Hawthorne, *The Scarlet Letter* (Boston, MA: Ticknor, Reed & Fields, 1850).

33. J. A. Cox, "Bilboes, Brands, and Branks," *Colonial Williamsburg Journal*, retrieved from http://www.history.org/Foundation/journal/spring03/branks.cfm.

34. Ibid.

35. Ibid.

36. Ibid.

37. Ibid.

38. Foucault, *Discipline and Punish*.

39. Ibid.

40. Ibid.

41. H. E. Allen, E. J. Latessa, and B. S. Ponder, *Corrections in America: An Introduction* (Boston, MA: Prentice Hall, 1998).

42. Roberts, J. W. (1997). *Reform and retribution: An illustrated history of American prisons*. Baltimore, MD: United Book Press

43. Allen, Latessa, and Ponder, *Corrections in America*.

44. K. Hall, and D. S. Clark, *The Oxford Companion to American Law* (New York, NY: Oxford University Press, 2002).

45. Foucault, *Discipline and Punish.*

46. Rossi as cited by Foucault, *Discipline and Punish.*

47. Allen, Latessa, and Ponder, *Corrections in America.*

48. Served 1930–1937.

49. Allen, Latessa, and Ponder, *Corrections in America.*

50. Ibid.

51. Ibid.

52. Ibid.

53. Hall and Clark, *The Oxford Companion to American Law.*

54. Pew Charitable Trust, 2011.

55. Hall and Clark, *The Oxford Companion to American Law.*

56. Ibid.

57. Federal Bureau of Prisons, "About Our Facilities," retrieved from http://www.bop.gov/about/facilities/federal_prisons.jsp.

58. Ibid.

59. Ibid.

60. Ibid.

61. Pew Charitable Trust, "State of Recidivism: The Revolving Door of America's Prisons," April 12, 2011, retrieved from http://www.pewtrusts.org/~/media/legacy/up-loadedfiles/wwwpewtrustsorg/reports/sentencing_and_corrections/StateRecidivism-RevolvingDoorAmericaPrisons20pdf.pdf.

62. U.S. Census Bureau, "U.S. and World Population Clock," retrieved 2014 from http://www.census.gov/popclock/.

63. "Incarceration," The Sentencing Project, retrieved from http://www.sentencingproject.org/template/page.cfm?id=107.

64. "Criminal Justice Fact Sheet," NAACP, retrieved http://www.naacp.org/pages/criminal-justice-fact-sheet.

65. D. T. Hutcherson, "Crime Pays: The Connection between Time in Prison and Future Criminal Earnings," *The Prison Journal*, June 19, 2012. DOI: 10.1177/0032885512448607.

66. Ibid.

67. Ibid.

68. Ibid.

69. S. Vedantam, "When Crime Pays: Prison Can Teach Some to Be Better Criminals," Nation Public Radio, retrieved from http://www.npr.org/2013/02/01/169732840/when-crime-pays-prison-can-teach-some-to-be-better-criminals.

70. C. W. Harlow, *Education and Correctional Populations* (Washington, D.C.: U.S. Department of Justice, 2003, p. 3).

THREE

Endow, Judge, and Accept

The Power and Morality of the Institution

The power institutions wield cannot be denied, but how institutions use, create, and endow power and morality to their dependents can often be mysterious. Schools and prisons have a reciprocal relationship as institutions and between the institutions and the communities in which they reside. This chapter discusses Erving Goffman's concept of the total institution, the institutions' role in creating power stratifications, and finally the effect that these concepts have on our communities.

In his groundbreaking book, *Asylums,* Erving Goffman coined the term *total institution* and identified four distinct features that make a total institution: (1) total institutions make dependents work, eat, and sleep within the same space; (2) every dependent's life takes place within the intimate company of others; (3) all activities are tightly scheduled; (4) all activities aim to fulfill the mission of the institution.[1] By Goffman's definition, total institutions are so named because the institution blurs the distinctive lines between places where people work, play, sleep, and eat. When given options, the majority of people chose to perform these actions in different locations; those within total institutions are not given a choice.

Five different types of institutions fulfill Goffman's requirements for a total institution.[2] The first type of total institution is the institution that cares for harmless people who are incapable of caring for themselves. These institutions include homes for the blind, elderly, orphaned, or homeless. The second type of institution cares for people who are a threat to the community and are not able to be left alone; currently, mental hospitals are the only type of institution in this category still in existence. The third type of total institution protects society from those who wish to cause harm. Institutions that currently fall under this category include jails, prisons, prisoner of war camps, and political prisons. The fourth type of institution is formed around a work-like task or training; Goffman likens these to the military or boarding schools. Lastly, is the institution that serves as an alternative space from society, like monasteries, convents, and abbeys.

In today's society, modern public schools fit the loose definition of Goffman's total institution. Schools today are required to provide students with nutritious food, safe places to learn, a place to play, and a place to work; by Goffman's definition, modern schools are only missing the residency aspect of a total institution. While modern schools are not all-encompassing institutions, they have many of the same components that total institutions contain. Goffman identified three worlds that exist within the total institution. Within the institution these worlds help the dependents and staff exist and function to the best of their abilities.

The first world that Goffman examines is the dependent world.[3] Although the total institution controls its dependents, dependents have their own world within the institution. Dependents are not just born; the institution, the staff, and older dependents create the new dependent. This dependent-making process has nine parts, not all of which are used in every institution or scenario. The first step in making a dependent is placing barriers between the dependent's former life on the outside of the total institution and his or her new life within the institution. For most students, this first step occurs when children are sent to preschool to get them ready for school. Other barriers between the home life of a student and school include fences designating school property and entry protocols, language barriers, surveillance, and metal detectors.

Once the barriers between the dependent's old life and new life are in place, the second step begins. This second step is the admissions procedures or programming. Programming involves the staff taking the life histories, pictures, weight, height, and fingerprints of the dependent, while assigning the dependents their numbers, cataloguing former personal items, issuing new institutional clothing, and assigning institutional space to the dependent. The admission process for schools entails children's kindergarten assessments, family information, and any information deemed important to the educational success of the child. Many student files include a photo of the student; his or her height, weight, and educational track; and notes from teachers about their perceptions of the child's abilities. Children are assigned a desk and a locker, their designated space within the institution.

Initiation is the next step in the dependent-making process. The point of initiation according to Goffman is to enforce the new lowly position of the dependent within the institution through communal possessions, initiation rituals, and obedience to the staff. Initiation in schools occurs when students enter the school and are immediately confronted by the unknown. This unknown places them at the bottom of the social structure, where they must learn the rules and norms of the school. Students are also forced to use communal bathrooms, showers, and spaces, which further enforce their position within the institution.

Along with the initiation rituals, personal defacement and disfigurement can occur. Personal defacement is considered the stripping of the self, of the control of oneself, and of the physical possessions and freedom of personal time schedules that dependents have before they enter the total institution.[4] Now they have to live under a schedule not their own. Personal disfigurement includes branding, beatings, loss of extremities, shock treatments, therapy, and surgery, so that dependents are marked with the brand of the institution permanently.[5] Although most schools have not used physical punishment in years, at one time, schools did use corporal punishment as a way to ensure students' good behavior, and several states still allow corporal punishment in schools.

The first three parts focus on the dependent and the stripping of his or her previous identity. Parts six through nine of the dependent-making process focus on how the dependent is made to accept his or her new identity. Part six of the process is the loss of the dependent's identity equipment, which includes certain movements, postures, and stances.[6] In schools, this is done through requiring students to raise their hands to be called on and to wear uniforms. These movements signal deference to others and help to convey the new lowly position of the student. Verbal humiliation is the seventh part of the process and this can include calling staff *sir* or *ma'am,* or having to ask for menial necessities like a drink of water or to use the restroom. The eighth part of the process occurs when students are subjected to indignities of treatment by others.[7] Indignities by others can include staff or other students cursing at, teasing, tormenting, constantly correcting mistakes, or gossiping about the student.

Mortification is the last part of the dependent-making process and occurs in two parts. The first type of mortification occurs when the dependent is forced to undertake a daily process that is unknown and unfamiliar. Student mortification can happen when students are forced into a new routine or pushed out of their comfort zones. There are two types of mortification Goffman calls "contaminative exposure," which have five subtypes.[8] Goffman explains contaminative exposure: "On the outside, the individual can hold actions, his thoughts, and some of his possessions—clear of contact with alien and contaminating things. But in total institutions these territories of the self are violated; the boundary that the individual places between his being and the environment is invaded and embodiments of self profaned."[9] Once inside the total institution, the dependent's space is constantly being touched and invaded by other dependents.

The first type of contaminative exposure is the violation of informational preserve.[10] Violation of informational preserve means that institutional staff knows information that dependents wish they knew, but do not have access to. This could include information about future grades, letters of notifications to parents, personal file information, and attendance records. The second type of contaminative exposure occurs when new audiences are able to learn information about dependents that dependents themselves would normally conceal. [11] For example, this type of contaminative exposure occurs when an outside institution like a counseling service or juvenile facility obtains information about a student. The school is required to turn over all relevant information even if the student may not normally divulge that information to a stranger.

The third type of contaminative exposure is physical. This can include "complaints about unclean food, messy quarters, soiled towels, shoes, and clothing impregnated with previous users' sweat, toilets without seats, and dirty bath facilities." [12] Although many schools maintain a level of cleanliness, budget constraints and falling tax bases have caused many schools to fall into disrepair. Jonathon Kozol's book, *Savage Inequalities*, details more about the conditions of schools as he found them on his cross-country journey in 1988.

The fourth type of contaminative exposure is medication and food. [13] Sometimes dependents attempt to exert minimal control by rejecting the food within the institution or medication that they are required to take. In instances like these, staff are required to force-medicate a dependent, both for the good of the dependent and to meet the institutional mission and rules. Interpersonal contamination, the last type of contaminative exposure, can be extreme or benign. [14] The extreme type of interpersonal contamination is molestation or rape, and the benign form can be the touching of a dependent's belongings by other dependents whom the owner considers undesirable. Unfortunately, schools have had issues with both types of interpersonal contamination, from teachers raping students to theft of students' personal possessions.

This dependent-making process is one of the first things encountered by the dependent within his or her new world. It becomes a rite of passage that must be gone through to become a part of the institution. While this dependent-making process may vary from institution to institution, it also changes based on whether entry into the institution is voluntary or involuntary.

Unfortunately, school attendance is now mandatory in all fifty states, so many students enter schools involuntarily. Some students easily become part of the institution, adapting and finding comfort and success in the policies, procedures, and routines that encompass the schools. Other students find that school is an uncomfortable place, an alien world with rules and language that is foreign and difficult to understand and follow. For students in this latter category, school is a place that makes them angry, anxious, defiant, or upset, as they balk against the rules and dependent-making process that all students are put through. Once these students are identified, normally through their behavior, they are often categorically labeled, and this label then follows them from teacher to teacher, year to year, and institution to institution, causing teachers to have preformed ideas about how the student will act or what he or she can accomplish.

All schools attempt to make children into students; children are often thought of as messy, uncivilized, disorderly, and unpredictable. Students, unlike children, are clean, civilized, orderly, and predictable; this is because school has groomed them to understand the rules, obey the rules, or face punishment. How many times have you asked a teacher what grade he or she teaches and when the response is kindergarten, you kindly tell the teacher how amazing he or she must be because you could never do what that teacher does? What exactly do kindergarten teachers do that is so amazing? Well, they take those messy, loud, chaotic children and teach them how to raise their hands, sit quietly, take turns, ask permission, and become a student.

Schools then take the students who have successfully managed to become the correct type of student and teach them the skills to become productive citizens.[15] These students adapt to the dependent-making process and the policies and procedures of the institution, often sailing through school with few problems and goals of attaining more education. For students who do not adapt to the dependent-making process, school is a struggle. These students disobey the policies and procedures of the school, causing the students to have more encounters with the punishment aspect of school.

These frequent clashes between the student and school normally result in the student having a negative attitude about school. Since these students are expelled or suspended frequently or for long periods, delinquent students habitually fall behind in their academic progress. Occasionally, this is due to learning disorders that are not diagnosed because the student is not in school long enough for the teacher or staff to realize there is a problem. Other times, the student falls behind simply because he or she is gone for such long periods that he or she misses too much material. When these students do reenter school, they are so far behind their peers that catching up seems like an insurmountable challenge. To many of these students, dropping out becomes the perfect way to escape an institution they see as uncaring, unfriendly, antiquated, and punitive.

For deviant students in schools with police officers or resource officers, the outcome of bad behavior can be dire, placing a student on a path from which there is little recourse. A physical disagreement can be viewed as an assault, a verbal altercation a threat; a wide variety of other issues that used to be handled by the school are now considered police matters and can result in criminal records for students. For those who do become incarcerated, the dependent-making process is once again repeated; however, this time, the process creates a prison inmate. Once an inmate is created, it is incredibly difficult to overcome the process of the institution.

In contrast to the first part of the total institution, the dependent world, the second part of the total institution is the staff world. The staff world has unique qualities that set staff apart from the dependents. Whereas dependents do not have status or relationships outside of the total institutions, staff have lives that continue outside of the institution.[16] In education, teachers' and administrators' lives outside of the school have been subjected to the scrutiny of the communities in which they reside. For example, Stacy Snyder, a student at Millersville University School of Education and a student teacher at Conestoga High school in Lancaster, Pennsylvania, was denied her teaching certificate days before graduation after posting a photo of herself to her Myspace page that showed her wearing a pirate costume and holding a red cup.[17] When she sued, claiming denial of her First Amendment rights, a federal judge ruled against her, citing that since she was a public employee and the matter concerns only private issues she had no standing to claim violation of her First Amendment rights.

This fearful precedent means that teachers and administrators are held to a higher standard in their personal lives than others. In schools, where staff work closely with students every day, bonds develop between staff and students. These bonds can give students the extra motivation needed to do well at school, or they can become a hindrance, leading to dysfunctional relationships between teachers and students.[18] This is especially true in high schools, where sometimes only a few years of age separate teachers from their students.

Staff within total institutions must also maintain humane standards for the dependents they control; within total institutions, dependents can take on the characteristics of inanimate objects.[19] Staff are given the responsibility to ensure that dependents are treated humanely while completing the paper trail that must follow each dependent. This paper trail ensures that the dependent is meeting the goals of the community and the institution. Internal supervisors, watchdogs, and society monitor these paper trails, as well as the behavior of the staff to make sure that the staff perform their job humanely and efficiently.

Maintaining humane standards in schools is less difficult than inside prisons, especially since students and staff both leave the institution and spend time within their home communities. However, a danger that is prevalent inside schools that is not present within prisons is the ability to delude ourselves into thinking that when our students leave the school, they all go to a place that is safe and warm, has food and the students' best interest at heart. Since most teachers enter the teaching profession to make a difference or because they excelled at school, it is often difficult for them to see school in the way some of their less fortunate students view schools. For students who are worried about their parent (or guardian) dying of a drug overdose, where their next meal might come from, or where their younger siblings might safely sleep the following night, the material covered in school does not seem as relevant as the need to survive.

While teachers are not millionaires by any means, most live a comfortable existence. They receive a regular paycheck, have the means to feed their families, and have the ability to live in a safe neighborhood. This disconnect between the realities of teachers and students can cause frustration for the teacher when students do not pay attention, make mistakes, or are unable to learn material. Since schools are expected to run as orderly machines and penalize those who fail, a student who has difficulty learning but no obvious learning problems can cause teachers and schools to be penalized, leading to frustration, a lack of empathy, and anger.[20]

Supervision is required because staff are often forced to choose between what is best for an individual dependent versus what is best for the entire group or what is best for the institution.[21] Staff implement the rules of the institution through threats, rewards, and punishments. Unfortunately, with the emphasis on testing and achievement, the focus on what is best for the institution versus what is best for the individual has become all too common. Testing has meant that schools and their students can be compared with other schools and other students, allowing schools to be graded on their ability to educate students. While those in education know that standardized tests are not an ideal or even a good way to compare students' knowledge and teachers' ability to teach, the public and government officials have latched onto testing as the panacea for all that ails education.

Few may realize that testing scores are published in local newspapers, comparing all schools in the area and their grades. Schools are even issued report cards allowing these testing scores and other variables to decide whether a school is successful at educating their students. This focus on the institutional grade of a school and the media hype that surrounds it means that teachers are forced to threaten, punish, and reward students for the ability to perform well on tests rather than their ability to learn. Pressure on schools have resulted in some underperforming schools resorting to cheating to avoid sanctions.

Testing scandals have surfaced in Georgia, Texas, Washington, D.C., Connecticut, Pennsylvania, Alabama, and many other states.[22] Right now, schools lack the same standardized supervision that prisons have; schools have the freedom to choose how they implement and monitor their tests and most districts have the power to investigate any wrongdoing that they believe may have occurred. However, the incentive to check for cheating on these tests is slim, especially in school districts where students struggle. In this manner, many schools have placed the welfare of the institution over the welfare of the individual.

Between the dependents' world and the staff world lie the formal and informal set of rules that introduce the inmate to the institution. Goffman lists three types of formal structures as part of these instructions: first are the house rules, second are the rewards and privileges, and third are the punishments.[23] Goffman defines house rules as "a relatively explicit and formal set of prescriptions and proscriptions that lays out the main requirements of inmate conduct."[24] Rewards and privileges are "held out in exchange for obedience to staff in action and spirit" and can be simple things that an inmate would take for granted in the outside world.[25] Finally, punishments "are designated as the consequence of breaking the rules."[26] These formal structures are written down and institution administration makes sure that staff enforces the instruction among the inmates.

The house rules for the school are issued by the school district, while teachers institute their own rules, as well as privileges and punishments for their classrooms. Teacher education programs focus on the theories of learning, leaving classroom control to be learned on the job. Research shows that teachers are in charge of a delicate balancing act that includes classroom management, student socialization, and disciplinary interventions.[27] Since classrooms contain diverse student learning needs and personalities, teachers have been mandated to create a classroom that meets the needs of all students. To do this, teachers must have a management system in place that works to minimize distractions and stop meltdowns before they disrupt the lesson and the classroom.

Teachers are not trained in this balancing act; it is either something that they intrinsically know how to do, or they learn through experience. Teachers must learn about both the formal rules and the "*heuristics* (implicit rules of thumb)."[28] Since the teacher is the instrument through whom the rules of the institution and the classroom are administered, the teacher is the link between the student and the institution.

Although the school itself is an institution, it is important to remember that the classroom, although part of the larger institution, is also its own miniature institution. Rules are applied from the larger institution, but there are also rules that apply only to the classroom. Students affect teachers, teachers affect students, formal and informal rules influence these interactions, and social and environmental factors all contribute to the complex system of the classroom.[29] Prison units and classrooms function as mini-institutions with their own complex social systems, but also as part of the larger social institutional system.

Total institutions thrive on creating atmospheres that are uniform and consistent, which allow them to meet their institutional missions and maintain better control. To do this, total institutions rely on their staff to be trained to follow and interpret orders with little deviation. Education, however, encourages its teachers to rely on their instincts when they feel something is problematic or wrong. This means that instead of having a consistent and uniform frame of reference for problems, schools are inundated with a variety of problems. For example, one teacher may send a student to the principal for refusing to quiet down in the classroom. Another teacher may handle the same situation by sending the offending student into the hallway. Classroom rules vary from teacher to teacher. One teacher might allow gum chewing and the teacher in the room next door might consider gum chewing a flagrant rule violation. These varying responses by representatives of the institution can be problematic, sending mixed messages to the students inside the institution.

This disconnect between consistency can lead to students using their social networks and power to display behavior that is detrimental to classroom management.[30] Students and their social networks can have more control in the classroom than the teacher. For example, McFarland writes of an observation he made during his fieldwork where he "witnessed students openly joking about how low their grades were."[31] Depending on the opinions and strength of the students, formal and informal protocols can be used as a bonding tool or they can be used to make a mockery of their intent.

A good friend of mine uses the following story when she teachers her undergraduate class at a local university: When she was a junior in her education program, her class was assigned a professor who on the first day of class walked in, broke the class up into groups, and assigned each group a chapter to present on from the book. Her classmates, being eager and avid future teachers, took their assignment seriously and created fabulous PowerPoint presentations, complete with interactive lessons for the class. The professor rewarded their hard work by falling asleep during their presentations. At first, the class thought it might be a fluke; after all, professors are people too. However, during the second, third, and fourth presentations, the professor continued to fall asleep.

The class was beginning to get angry that their hard work was being ignored and disregarded so blatantly by a person who would later be assigning them grades. Although the class worried and discussed their situation outside of class, they were reluctant to take any action until they had more solid evidence. This solid evidence came during the second exam; the professor walked into the class, distributed the tests and left. This followed the exact same protocol as the first test. Grades on the first test had ranged from a 50 to a 100 with no feedback; the grades appeared arbitrary and confusing. The test required short answers and when the class compared their answers, they found that all were similar. The class began to suspect that the grades were based on whether the professor liked the student.

When the professor dropped the second set of tests on the desk and left, a discussion ensued among the students. The discussion focused on how the class could complete their tests with similar answers, but not cheat. Their answer came in the form of taking a group test, but creating answers that were similar but not exact. Question by question, the entire class discussed and answered the test. When the tests were given back, the grades once again had a huge range with no justifications or information. When the class asked the professor, he told them that he was the sole decider of the grades and that no one should question his decision.

For this group of teacher candidates, that moment proved to be a vital lesson in how not to lead a classroom. From that moment, the entire class bonded together to take over the class from the professor. They continued to create interactive lessons and use the class to model their future teaching behaviors, but the professor had almost no control of the actual class. At one point, the professor attempted to regain control of the classroom, but the class no longer took him seriously. The class had taken over the weak instrument of the institution, the professor, and his lack of implementation of the rules, and hijacked the classroom. This class, from the moment that it existed, had broken the chain of the total institution. If this had happened in a public high school, the consequences could have been far reaching. Imagine the chaos if kindergarteners ran the school or prison inmates ran the prison.

The image of kindergarteners running a school or prison inmates running the prison may seem humorous, especially since these institutions hold such power within the community and the nation. Schools serve not only as places to educate the children of the community, but as a place where the community shows its pride. Take, for example, schools with a successful program. This program could be academic or athletic, but once a school demonstrates its success in a specific area, the community normally rallies around the school and the program. An example of this is high school football; most communities, especially in Ohio where I grew up, are incredibly proud of their high school football programs.

It does not matter if the program has only won two games in the last twenty years. Football often brings out the community support. In my hometown, every Friday during football season there is a pep rally to support the team. Before kickoff, a long line of cars can be seen attempting to find parking at the school and the stadium begins to fill with community members. Many supporters are wearing the school colors and holding signs showing their support for their favorite team. Visiting fans compete with the home crowd to show their support for their team. Even people without children in the school district attend the game to show their support for their school.

In this way, the program, which could range from football to orchestra, brings community support to the school. This support is powerful; communities that have lost their school, decline.[32] Many different results have been shown in the research; some results have shown that communities are already in decline before schools have been consolidated or closed; other research shows that schools affect community vitality.[33] In many communities, the school is the major employer within the community as well as the gathering place. The relationship between schools and communities are symbiotic; communities rely on the economic input from the school and schools depend on the taxes that community members pay.[34]

Prisons have capitalized on many rural communities, attempting to create the same symbiotic relations that schools and communities have created. Finding a location to construct a new prison is difficult; many communities are reluctant or dead set against allowing prisons entry into the community. To combat this reluctance, prisons began targeting rural areas, citing the economic advantages that can be brought to the community with the construction of the prison. Prison proponents use the lure of new job creation to convince many rural and economically depressed areas that accepting a new prison within their space would boost economic prosperity.[35] Many struggling rural towns embrace this information and accept prisons, believing that local people will be hired as correctional officers and staff for the new prison. In a manner of speaking, the prisons follow the schools' example, but with far different results.

The exact effect of prisons on communities is hard to pinpoint, but rarely have they achieved all that they have promised. Many community members believe that prisons will create full-time jobs that disappeared when manufacturing or farming left. Most employment offered in depressed economic areas before the arrival of the prison is part-time, lacking benefits, or room for growth.[36] Politicians and prison officials herald prisons as an opportunity to provide careers and solid employment. Similar to schools, prison jobs and management positions are only available to those with specific educational experiences, which deny many community members the opportunity to find employment at the prison.[37] However, schools are able to offer community members outside positions, such as janitorial work, coaching positions, bus drivers, and other tertiary work. Prisons, because of their self-contained nature, offer almost no external opportunities for community members.

Despite these broken promises, selecting a site for a prison requires a competitive bidding process.[38] Since many politicians and political leaders tout prisons as a way to bring economic growth to depressed areas, to be competitive in the bidding market, many communities offer necessary services at reduced prices, using these reductions as incentives for selection.[39] Communities can use reduced sewer, water, and electric prices to lure prison construction; in New York in 1996, Governor Pataki's proposal to build three new prisons caused one small town that hoped to secure the contract to apply for a 600,000 dollars federal grant to improve their water supply system.[40] Other towns, desperate for jobs, have built prisons and then invited private corporations to run them. Three towns in Oklahoma secured over 34 million dollars from investors, built the prisons, and invited the private firm Corrections Corporation of America to oversee the new institutions.[41]

A study funded by the Center for Rural Pennsylvania examined the perceptions of community members and state prison officials near four Pennsylvania prisons. Based on the research, the authors suggested thirteen improvements that the Department of Corrections in Pennsylvania should implement.[42] Of these thirteen suggestions, enhanced communication with the surrounding community was evident in two suggestions; more contracts with local business was also emphasized, as was a suggestion for hiring more local community members and a call for transparency and honesty about the economic effect of the prison in the community.[43]

Simplified, this tradeoff embraces prisons as the new economic savior of schools, a troubling notion. If prisons are the archetype of the total institution and schools are closely following the model, what does this say about our mentality toward the children we educate? This creation by the school of the dependent or good citizen brings about a troubling issue. If schools are tasked with creating good citizens through the dependent-making process, schools are also creating morality and dispensing power.

By rewarding those who abide by school rules, schools emphasize that the behavior that they require is the behavior of good citizens. When students who disobey school rules are punished, students who follow the rules are taught that those being punished are bad, a designation of morality. In fact, the language used to describe these types of students, *good* or *bad,* is both a description of power and morality. Once good students are rewarded by the school for successfully completing the dependent-making process, this good versus bad morality follows the former student outside the school, creating a sense of power in the community.

This morality is then used to judge the actions of others, based on prior experiences during their time in school, and often those who were successful at school hold positions of power. Here is an illustration from one of my college classes. As a graduate student, I sat in on an undergraduate criminology course. The class demographic was composed of mostly male students, with many wanting to go onto careers in law enforcement. Our professor, a wise and seasoned veteran of the prison system, divided us into groups and handed each of us a small sheet of paper.

On that sheet of paper was a story about a man. The man had gotten caught with a small amount of marijuana on his person, intended for personal use only. From there, the story detailed more about his personal life; he was a high school dropout who had lost his job in a factory. His wife had divorced him and taken the children, and currently he was searching for meaningful employment but suffering from nightmares, anxiety, and lack of an education. Our group was to discuss his case and sentence him appropriately, and then compare our sentences with the class. The entire class decided in their groups to throw the proverbial book at the man, sentencing him to five to ten years in prison.

At this moment, I realized that everyone in the room had projected their similar version of morality onto this man to label him as bad, and then proceeded to use their power to punish him. When I suggested that with more education and a drug treatment facility this man could become a productive member of the community, my response was met with the reply that he needed to be punished for breaking the law. Treatment and education were not considered punishment. From that moment forward, I became concerned about how we consciously and subconsciously educate our students about morality and power in schools. Therefore, we must ask whether we are comfortable and approving of the messages of morality and power that emanate from our schools. If we are, then why are we so discontented with the rising number of incarcerations?

NOTES

1. E. Goffman, *Asylums: Essays on the Social Situation of Mental Patients and Other Inmates* (Garden City, NY: Anchor Books, 1961).

2. Ibid.

3. Goffman calls this world the "Inmate World"; however, for the purpose of this chapter, since we are discussing schools, I have replaced *inmate* with *dependent,* since both depend on the institution to provide basic necessities.

4. Goffman, *Asylums.*

5. I am not sure how relevant this is to total institutions today. Laws have been passed that protect those within total institutions; however, it may still be relevant in total institutions that are joined voluntarily. An example could include a brand willingly put on the body of a fraternity brother to show his allegiance to the fraternity.

6. Goffman, *Asylums.*

7. Ibid.

8. Ibid.

9. Ibid.

10. Ibid.

11. Ibid.

12. Ibid.

13. Ibid.

14. Ibid.

15. "Correct type" here is a generalization or stereotype, but one that is encountered often. The correct type of student is one who behaves according to the rules and willingly does his or her work with little question.

16. Goffman, *Asylums.*

17. Snyder v. Millersville University et al. Civil Action No. 07-1660. Dec. 3, 2008 U.S District Court, E.D. Pennsylvania 2008 WLS093140.

18. The most famous example of this type of dysfunctional relationship is Mary Kay LeTourneau, now Mary Kay Faulaau, who had a relationship and children with her (at the time) 12-year-old student. After LeTourneau served prison time, they are now married. However, there are other examples of this type of dysfunctional relationship, featuring both male and female teaches.

19. Goffman, *Asylums.*

20. This is not a criticism of teachers. It is a criticism of how education is run today. With an emphasis on testing, scores, and specific achievement ratings, there is little time to focus on the personal needs of students outside of the classroom.

21. Goffman, *Asylums.*

22. Becket, 2013; Sanchez, 2013; Rich & Hurde, 2014; Toppo, 2011

23. Goffman, *Asylums.*

24. Ibid.

25. Ibid.

26. Ibid.

27. J. Brophy, "Educating Teachers about Managing Classrooms and Students," *Teaching and Teacher Education* 4, no. 1 (1988): 1–18.

28. Ibid.

29. E. Cohen, "Sociology and the Classroom: Setting the Conditions for Teacher-Student Interaction," *Review of Educational Research* 42, no. 4 (1972): 441–452.

30. D. A. McFarland, "Student Resistance: How the Formal and Informal Organization of Classrooms Facilitate Everyday Forms of Student Defiance," *American Journal of Sociology* 107, no. 3 (2001): 612–678.

31. McFarland, "Student Resistance," 623-624.

32. R. S. Sell, F. L. Leistritz, and J. M. Thompson, *Socio-economic Impacts of School Consolidation on Host and Vacated Communities,* North Dakota Department of Agricultural Economics Report 347, 1996.

33. Bard, Gardener, & Wieland, 2005; Lyson, 2002; Purcell & Shackleford, 2005.

34. While *symbiotic* is normally used in science to described a long-term relationship between two different species, in this case, the community is viewed as one species, the school as another.

35. T. Huling, "Building a Prison Economy in Rural America," in *From Invisible Punishment: The Collateral Consequence of Mass Imprisonment,* eds. M. Mauer, M. Chesney-Lind (New York: New York Press, 2002).

36. Ibid.

37. Ibid.

38. Ibid.

39. Ibid.

40. Ibid.

41. Ibid.

42. K. Courtright, M. Hannan, S. Packard, and E. Brennan, "Prisons and Rural Pennsylvania Communities: Exploring the Health of the Relationship and the Possibility of Improvement," *The Prison Journal* 90, No. 1 (2010): 69–93.

43. Ibid.

FOUR

Special Education or Prison Sentence

There are many dirty little secrets in education, but one of the most dangerous is a secret that no one is discussing. No one is talking about the role special education plays in creating a class of students who are more suited for prison than for college. Before immediate denial, read this chapter, talk to a school guidance counselor, and think deeply about how your school handles students with special needs. This is not about blame; teachers and administrators normally do the best job that they possibly can with the resources that are available to them. This chapter highlights the problem with the structure of special education. In trying to help the most vulnerable and needy students, we may actually be hurting them more than we know.

To have this conversation, it is important to understand how the special education process works. While each state has nuances within their special education programs, federal law mandates the majority of the process. This means that most of the special education processes would look the same in Ohio, Montana, Arizona, Louisiana, or wherever you are located. It is important that we understand how it is determined that a student needs special education services. The following procedures describe what happens for every student who has a suspected disability. There are obviously slight variations depending on the state and the student's suspected disability.

Identifying a student with special needs is not always the easiest task. Large classrooms, chaotic schedules, daily demands, and a host of other responsibilities can distract a teacher from the signs that a student is struggling with more than just homework. In the majority of cases, parents bring their concerns to the guidance counselor, principal, or teacher citing trouble with homework, inability to pay attention, apparent lack of learning, or other issues. Occasionally, teachers recognize that students are having problems and refer them to the guidance counselor's office or special education office for evaluations. Other public agencies and out-side personnel, such as Children's Services, doctors, social workers, and psychologists are also able to recommend that students be tested for learning disabilities or other special needs.

Referrals for testing to see if a student qualifies for a special education diagnosis are directed to the guidance or special needs department with-in a school. After a student receives a referral, the guidance counselor or supervisor meets with the student's teachers and parents to gather infor-mation. Teacher interventions and observations, classroom situations, discussions with parents, discipline records, and any other information that is pertinent for evaluating the problem is collected from all parties. Using the collected documentation, teachers, parents, and guidance counselors attempt to put plans into place that will help the student find success. Teachers are gathered together and their attempts at interven-tions are discussed. A Building Level Assistance Team (BLAT) meeting is scheduled that includes the student's parents or guardians, one of the student's teachers, and any outside agencies that have contact with the child. All information regarding the child, including input from doctors, counselors, and anyone with information relevant to the perceived prob-lem, is welcomed and given consideration.

This meeting has several different names.[1] The purpose of the BLAT meeting is to decide whether the student qualifies for testing for special education services when all else has failed or has not created the desired improvement. If the documentation presented at the BLAT meeting shows that the child does not need a Multi-Factored Evaluation (MFE) for special education qualification purposes, a plan must be put in place to address the student's issues. An MFE is a set of evaluations that are conducted to determine whether a student is eligible for special educa-tion services. Some of these evaluations include:

- vision
- hearing
- communication status (written expression, oral communication, and listening comprehension)
- intelligence
- achievement
- teacher observation
- social and emotional
- visual motor
- gross and fine motor
- adaptive behavior
- vocational evaluation skills
- psychological testing
- teacher input

- parent input
- disciplinary input

If a child is over the age of 14, a vocational evaluation must be completed in which skills used in the real world, such as punctuality, cleanliness, following directions, telling time, and other employability skills are assessed. One of the testing instruments that can be used is the Employability and Life Skills Assessment (ELSA). At the BLAT meeting, the successes and failures of the classroom interventions attempted by teachers are discussed, new interventions are thought out, timelines are named, and the emotional and physical health of the child is discussed. Essentially, the BLAT is done to give a snapshot of the child to the evaluation team. From this snapshot, the BLAT will decide if an MFE for special education qualification purposes is appropriate. If at the BLAT meeting there is consensus that other interventions need to be attempted before testing, the interventions are recorded on the intervention team form, along with a timeline and a reconvene date to discuss the success and failures of that particular intervention. Everything is documented.

Should the BLAT team decide that all possible classroom interventions have failed and it is appropriate to recommend the student for an MFE, parents or guardians must grant permission to the school district to proceed with the process. There are two ways for parents or guardians to grant this permission; one is through the mail and the other is in person. If the student is a ward of the state, then the agency having custody of the student must sign. These agencies or people could include Children's Services, the district-appointed surrogate for students without parents, or a guardian ad litem. Before permission can be granted, parents or others must receive the federal regulations for special education in a booklet titled *Whose IDEA Is This?*[2] A form called Prior Written Notice is filled out and sent to the parents. The facilitator of the BLAT team completes the Prior Written Notice form, which states the intention and the reasons of the team for creating the action plan, and the parents receive a planning sheet.

There is a planning sheet for elementary students and high school students, each of which lists all of the tests available. The purpose of the planning sheet is to inform parents about which evaluations their child will be receiving. For example, a high school student given an MFE with a suspected disability of a specific learning disability will be evaluated in the following areas:

- vision
- hearing
- communication status (written expression, oral communication, and listening comprehension)
- intelligence
- achievement

- teacher observation
- social and emotional
- visual motor
- gross and fine motor
- adapted behavior (as needed)

The adaptive behavior is the only one listed "as needed" because if during the testing by the school psychologist a cognitive delay is suspected, then the adaptive behavior evaluation must be completed. If a student faces limited English proficiency, further evaluations are needed. Once it is completed, the parents or guardians receive all of the paperwork and must return it signed and dated.

Once the school has received the signed permission to test and planning sheet, the facilitator of special education delegates the testing to the appropriate personnel. From the date on the permission to test form, the school has sixty days to complete the MFE and conduct the evaluation team meeting. This includes weekends, holidays, summer vacation, and leap year. Parents receive notification fourteen days before the meeting through the parent invitation form and are supposed to respond. If a parent does not respond, the meeting can be held, but a student's placement cannot be changed without parent permission.

At the MFE meeting, the following people must be present:

- school psychologist
- district representative
- teacher who can speak to the student's classroom abilities
- age-appropriate special education teacher
- parent

This is not an all-inclusive list; others with relevant data may be invited. Each of these people arrives with their data already prepared or presents their data to a team member to be reported.

Results of the testing are discussed, eligibility of the student is determined, and a team summary is compiled. Everyone at the meeting signs to verify that they attended the meeting; if there is dissention, a dissenting opinion must be written and presented within thirty days of the meeting to the facilitator of the evaluation team.

The purpose of the MFE team is to decide eligibility, not placement. Once eligibility is determined and if the child is eligible for placement in a special education program, the school has thirty days to determine the appropriate placement or placements, write an Individualized Education Plan (IEP) and enact it. The IEP is a working, binding, legal document that, at any time with a request from the parent or teacher, can be changed, but it must be reviewed annually from the date it was written. The MFE is conducted every three years to determine if the special education placement continues to be appropriate.

With a placement in special education, the goal of educators is to create a support system that will help the student succeed. Teachers and administrators normally define success as graduating and receiving a diploma from high school. What happens if the special education structures that we put into place are a hindrance for the student? In the case of Matthew, a labeling of special education originally helped him overcome his learning disability, but later put him in contact with other students in special education who found social acceptance in drug usage.

In fourth grade, Matthew was referred to the guidance counselor for acting out in class and causing disruption every moment of the day. No matter what the teacher tried, nothing interested Matthew. Finally, after several failed intervention attempts, the teacher recommended that Matthew receive special education testing. The information collected from the teachers and others surrounding Matthew pointed to a gifted and talented identification.

During the MFE, the school psychologist found that Matthew had an IQ of 146, which put him in the genius status, but he was only achieving at the average range, which is between 90 and 109. These big discrepancies, especially in English and written language, made him eligible for special education in the categories of specific learning disabilities. Matthew was kept in his mainstream classes with inclusionary help, including modifications. Modifications inside his normal classroom as well as pullout classes provided Matthew with the academic boost that he needed. His grades began to improve and his behavior problems ceased temporarily.

Unlike many special education students, Matthew did not display social issues facilitated by his label of special education. He was popular, well liked, socially adept, now earned good grades, and had made vast improvements in his deficit areas. However, this popularity became a problem for Matthew. As his grades improved, his confidence swelled and he become socially aware that he was smarter than the students surrounding him. Matthew had one pullout class, Reading and Study Skills, where he was exposed to students who had similar disabilities but fewer social skills. Some of those students, who suffered exclusion from peer groups within school because of their social awkwardness, had found acceptance on the streets with the local drug culture. While the excluded students found drugs as an escape from peer ostracism, Matthew saw drugs as a way to expand his mind, believing that he could control his usage because of his superior intelligence.

Matthew started using marijuana, but quickly moved onto harder drugs. By the time he was a junior in high school, he was into LSD and cocaine. Teachers and administrators suspected that he was coming to school high, but he was smart enough to avoid detection. Matthew's reading and English skills had improved dramatically, so much so that he was given the lead role in the school play, which required him to memorize and repeat large portions of the script. Matthew performed in the play, but received a three-day suspension after the play. The reason for the suspension stemmed from Matthew's drug use; with increasing drug usage, his behavior in class once again lapsed into the unacceptable range. He would sleep in class, exhibit erratic behavior, and presented an apathetic appearance; his schoolwork also suffered.

With his decline in school, a physical decline also occurred; he no longer resembled the successful, bright student that he once had been. The school contacted his mother and stepfather, but they felt that they could not help him either. Matthew barely graduated and has continued to deal and use drugs, but has not yet spent time in jail.

Matthew did not come from a lower class socioeconomic family. His family was middle class. His stepfather had been in the picture since Matthew was young, and home was a safe place. Matthew's sister, McKenna, who also had a superior level IQ did not have the behavioral or academic problems that Matthew faced. She graduated at the top of her class and enrolled in college. McKenna, like Matthew, was smart and popular, but unlike Matthew, she avoided the label of special education. Could this difference have played a role in their future paths?

While processing Matthew's story, let us switch institutions. Prison, the place that no one talks about unless they are forced to, may show us that what we are doing with students like Matthew is more damaging than socioeconomic status or educational attainment. The focus of this section is on the state and federal incarceration systems. Local jails run differently and are not in the scope of this research. First, a crime must be committed by a law-breaking citizen; this crime must violate either state or federal law for the felon to be eligible for sentencing in state or federal prison. Second, police must find and apprehend the correct person, who is given a chance to be proven innocent or guilty in a court of law. Once the court has made its decision, if the person is found guilty, the following processes begin.

Prisons intake systems work in a fashion similar to the special education process described previously. Initial designation follows the order that is laid out in the Program Statement: Inmate Security Designation and Custody Classification. Information that arises from the trial that is deemed important for sentencing is acquired by the Designation and Sentence Computation Center (DSCC), which enters it into the SENTRY system. Each inmate's records are computerized; guards, medical staff, and others with proper authority can access these records to gain a more comprehensive look at the inmate.

Once the information is in the SENTRY system, the DSCC uses the classification system to determine if the inmate needs central inmate monitoring (CIM), which attempts to anticipate the risks that the inmate poses to both the guards and the prison community. The DSCC Designation Officers also use SENTRY to help place inmates in the most appropriate facility. The SENTRY system provides information to the DSCC Designation Officers about the inmate population and capacity of each institution. SENTRY tells the DSCC Designation Officer how many inmates of each security level are currently housed in each facility. This allows DSCC Designation Officers to place new inmates in places that are able to meet their classification levels, CIM, and program needs.

After the completion of the initial designation by the DSCC Designator, all the documents are sent to the designated institution within two working days.[3] According to the Program Statement issued by the U.S. Department of Justice, which provides policy and procedures to the Bureau of Prisons in the United States, all inmates must be classified within twenty-eight days once they arrive at their assigned facilities.[4] This classification allows prison personnel to balance the security risks and program needs of the inmate. Once the inmate receives their placement, they undergo social, medical, and psychological services screenings. Prison personnel are looking for signs of mental illness, physical ailments or diseases, and social interactions skills. During this process staff attempt to determine if there are nonmedical reasons why the inmate should be housed away from the general population. The results are entered into the SENTRY system and are a deciding factor in the classification process.

Unit Teams handle two types of regularly scheduled meetings, Initial Classification meetings and Program Reviews. Unit Managers are in charge of making sure these meetings are scheduled at the appropriate time and meet all the requirements in the Program Statements. In Program Reviews, the progress in recommended programs for the inmates is reviewed. New programs are suggested based on the inmates' acquisition of new skills. These Program Reviews need to occur once every 180 calendar days.[5]

Initial Classification meetings normally take place while the inmate is housed in the Special Housing Unit. Delays should not be longer than two weeks after the originally scheduled meeting and the reasons for the delay should be noted on the SENTRY system.[6] The Initial Classification conference is to develop a plan for the inmate during his or her time of incarceration. According to the Program Statement, "This plan should include work and programming activities which will assist the inmate to develop skills to make a successful transition back into the community."[7] This meeting occurs within twenty-eight days of a new inmate's arrival at the facility, but this also happens when inmates transfer facilities, violate parole, disobey supervision or commit other violations that bring inmates back into the facility.

Each inmate is assigned a classification team; these teams include the inmate's assigned Unit Manager, a Case Manager, Correctional Counselor, an Education Advisor, and a psychological services counselor.[8] The Education Advisor is the team's consultant on education, recreation, and vocational matters relative to all the inmates in the unit. Target periods for program completion, measurable assessments, and participation fall under the jurisdiction of the Education Advisor. Additionally, the Education Advisor may be assigned to more than one team and may not be able to attend every meeting. Unit psychologists are also not required to attend every meeting, but they are responsible for providing the Unit Team with the written psychological reports for the new inmates. The medical staff completes an entire examination and enters the information on SENTRY so that the Unit Team can also have access to the information.

Each classification team member is responsible for bringing specific information to the Initial Classification conference. As the name states, the Unit Manager is the person responsible for scheduling the meeting, arranging the appearance of the inmate at the meeting and signing off on the SENTRY report. Contained in the SENTRY report are forms that give a snapshot of the inmate as a person to the classification team. Background information, history, family, health, education, and other forms are available to give team members a glimpse of the person before incarceration. When the Unit Manager signs off on the SENTRY report, he or she is certifying that all forms are current, the correct people were present, and the information contained in each form is correct to the best of his or her knowledge.

Case Managers are responsible for making sure the inmate appears at the classification meeting as well as providing a summary of the inmate's "current offense, prior record, social situation, security/custody classification, Financial Responsibility Program obligations, Release Preparation Program Participation, and other special programming considerations."[9] The Case Manager role is similar to the role of social worker; Case Managers have contact with the inmate's family, handle the majority of the inmate's paperwork, and are involved with the inmate's reentry into the community. Case Managers help to review the progress of the inmate in his or her assigned programs, and act as an advisor to the inmate on personal problems, employment issues, family problems, and institutional adjustment.

The last required member of the classification meeting is the Correctional Counselor. Correctional Counselors are responsible for informing the classification meeting about the inmate's work performance, participation in individual counseling or group counseling, general adjustment, and living quarter's sanitation. When the Education Advisor is unable to attend a unit team meeting, the Correctional Counselor provides a summary of the inmate's education test results, recommended educational program needs, and progress toward completion of education and other applicable release readiness programs.[10] A team docket, which contains the name, registered number, date, and time of each inmate's meeting is posted at least forty-eight hours prior to the meeting in a public place in the unit. The inmate can sign a waiver that voids the forty-eight-hour public posting, especially if the inmate does not have access to public areas.

Inmate attendance is expected at the Initial Classification; if all of the protocols are met and the inmate does not show up, disciplinary action is often taken. The absence of the inmate and the disciplinary action is then noted in the SENTRY system, as well as the reasons that the inmate has provided, if there is a reason provided. A copy is then forwarded to the inmate noting changes, classifications, reclassifications, time limits, performance levels, expected program accomplishments, and the inmates assigned work detail.[11] At the end of the unit meeting, a copy of the SENTRY Program Preview Report is filed in the Inmate Central File and a copy is also signed by the inmate. If the inmate dislikes the information in the SENTRY file, he or she has the right to appeal a decision made during Initial Classification.

Inmates are classified so that they can be placed in facilities that provide appropriate security and fit their program needs. There are five designated security levels for inmates—minimum, low, medium, high, and administrative—and classification is based on a point total that is determined by the Unit meeting team. These initial classifications are not solid; they are subject to change at any time during an inmate's period of incarceration.

With a general understanding of the two processes and the similarities between the two, let us look at why you should care. It is easy to read these descriptions and say to yourself, "Well, that is all well and fine, but there are a million other concerns: Adequate Yearly Progress (AYP), funding, and a thousand students, teachers, parents, and community members who need my direct attention," and you are correct—they do. However, there is a catch here. Although those concerns do need your attention and are critical, you have the unique ability to change the landscape in America without extra effort. To do this, we first need to look at who is at risk in schools and why they are at risk.

Students with special needs in schools have always had a tough time getting the help that they need to fit in socially and academically within schools. It was not until the passage of the Education for the Handicapped Act (EHA) in 1975 that students with disabilities and their parents were given a guarantee that these students would have access to a free and appropriate public education (FAPE).[12] The EHA said that appropriate education services needed to be provided at no cost to parents for students with disabilities. To do this, schools, especially special needs departments, were charged with testing and developing an IEP for each student with disabilities. An IEP, as briefly mentioned previously is a "plan based on multi-disciplinary assessment[s] and includes a statement of specific special education and related services to be provided to the child."[13] The EHA also introduced the term *least restrictive environment (LRE)* and said that students must be educated in the LRE for their disability. Under the EHA, parents were also given the right to participate in every decision made about their child, were required to sign off on every treatment suggested for their child, and had the right to due process should the requirements not be met.

In 1990, the EHA was changed to become the Individuals with Disabilities Education Act (IDEA) and added a few more requirements. Schools were now required to provide transition services for students older than the age of sixteen, broaden the definition of who was included in IDEA,[14] and include assistive technology devices and services in the IEP; LRE was also redefined.[15, 16] The year of 1997 saw three more changes to IDEA: LRE was extended to ensure that all students would have access to the general curriculum, assistive technology devices that were purchased by the school could be used by the student at home if not doing so interferred with FAPE, and other services were added for children who are blind or have visual impairments. What IDEA did not do for schools, however, was to add much needed funds to these new requirements. School districts were forced to implement these unfunded mandates, which proved to be a financial burden. This legislation without appropriate funding has created a situation for schools that is sometimes difficult to handle, especially for schools with large special education populations and limited resources.

In recent years, a scary trend has been emerging in special education; African-American and Hispanic boys are placed in special education at a rate almost twice that of White boys. African-American boys are more often diagnosed with mental retardation or a specific learning disability and placed in special education than White boys.[17] Once placed in special education, a variety of problems can develop. Anyone who works within schools knows that students form cliques. It is a fact that students feel a strong need to belong to an accepting group. Unfortunately, this means that students who are different, such as students with disabilities, are excluded from the school community. Therefore, students who already struggle with the academic side of school now face an additional hurdle of navigating the social world of school.

Generations of African-American and Hispanic boys are being put through the special education process. The diagnosing, sorting, categorizing, and then prescribed treatment for the disability familiarizes students with the labeling process. Once they obtain their label, these students carry this stigma with them for life. Regardless of what IDEA dictates, many of these students are shuttled into special classes that differentiate them from their peers. This ostracism often enhances the social difficulties that many students with disabilities face as peers ridicule and deride students for their perceived differences. Because these students do not fit into the social structure of schools, most attempt to find acceptance outside of the school. Once students are forced to find acceptance outside of the school, teachers and administrators no longer have the ability to intervene or help direct these students to healthier alternatives.

Patton argues that when schools diagnose a student as needing special education and then place them in a program that will help them academically, students miss the standard curriculum as well as the subtle social curricula that is taught.[18] Some argue that the answer to this problem is inclusion, where students with special needs are included in classrooms with their peers and offered modifications by teachers to address their specific needs. However, students that are mainstreamed often miss the concentrated and direct help offered in pullout classes. It seems that current special education classes leave the student in a place of limbo, caught between their non–special education peers and their special education peers. It can be an awkward position for both students with special needs and non–special education students.

Patton's article also looks at the overidentification of African American boys in special education. Patton brings to light that the identification "as mentally disabled has not changed much from 38 percent in 1975 when those students constituted 15 percent of the school population. In 1991 they made up 16 percent of this nation's school population and 35 percent of the special education population."[19] How is this possible? With the changes happening in special education between 1975 and 1991, how could almost nothing have changed? Is it possible that the system is broken or biased beyond repair?

Students are put into special education when there is a large gap between what they are capable of achieving and their actual achievement level. Patton found that "students, then, who fail in general education are viewed as defective and consequently as needing some 'special' system to organize itself, develop a different set of norms, values, roles, expectations and procedures to 'fix' these 'defective' students."[20] This is still the role that special education plays today. Students are placed into special education with the intention of fixing their achievement problems, but instead, they are socially isolated and labeled by teachers and peers. It can be little wonder that they turn to outside sources to find a peer group and acceptance.

Young African-American and Hispanic boys are especially at risk for turning to the streets looking for peer acceptance. Many of these young boys live in urban areas where the influence of gangs and the lure of the street promise much more than a classroom ever could. On the street as a low-level drug dealer, young men can handle hundreds of thousands of dollars in a week or so, earning only a small percentage of that cash, but enough to make them feel rich. For many of these young men, it is easier to find peer acceptance and make a living on the street than it is to complete school and find a minimum wage job. To African-American and Hispanic boys, staying in school offers no guarantees, but continues to expose them to ridicule, struggles, and only a slim chance of a better job. With no promises, few friends, and failing grades, most African-American and Hispanic boys find it hard to see the future promised in education.

The statistics on juvenile facilities are even more staggering. Approximately 34 percent of incarcerated students have a disability under IDEA compared to the 10 percent of the student population in public high schools[21]. Many released offenders do not return to complete high school. The emphasis in the juvenile system is on completing a general education diploma, but very few continue their education past the level of functional skills, if at all. However, disabilities do not only have to be academic. Social disabilities play a huge role in a juvenile's decision to go back to school after an incident with law enforcement.

In 2011, 1 in every 107 adults was incarcerated, which amounts to a total incarcerated population of 2,239,000.[22] Behind this statistic, however, are the stories of the inmates; not all stories are similar, but most have several common threads leading back to their time in school. A study conducted by Caroline Wolf Harlow, a statistician for the Bureau of Justice, found that most inmates had not graduated from high school, and that the number of inmates who had not graduated from high school increased from the 1991 survey at all levels of incarceration.

At the local level, inmates were asked deeper questions about their educational experiences. Inmates in jail were asked why they had not finished their high school education. Almost 35 percent (34.9 percent) of inmates at the local jail dropped out of high school due to behavioral or academic problems in school; compare this to the 17.2 percent of the general, nonincarcerated population. Many students who are at risk in school are dropping out and ending up incarcerated. Young inmates are in even more danger of not having attended any form of higher education. Harlow found that only 3.6 percent of inmates younger than the age of twenty-four had attended college, whereas 6.9 percent of those older

Table 4.1.

Educational Attainment	Total Incarcerated	State	Federal	Local Jail Inmates	Probationers	General Population
Some high school or less	41.3 percent	39.7 percent	26.5 percent	46.5 percent	30.6 percent	18.4 percent
GED	23.4 percent	28.5 percent	22.7 percent	14.1 percent	11.0 percent	...
High school diploma	22.6 percent	20.5 percent	27.0 percent	25.9 percent	34.8 percent	33.2 percent
Postsecondary	12.7 percent	11.4 percent	23.9 percent	13.5 percent	23.6 percent	48.4 percent

than forty-five were either college graduates or had attended some college.[23] Since so many young inmates are currently incarcerated for drug charges, looking at their education level is important. Forty-seven percent (46.6 percent) of those incarcerated for drug crimes had not graduated from high school. These numbers today are much higher; however, due to budget cutbacks, these studies are only conducted once every five years and the newest data have not been released. These numbers will only continue to rise as students, who feel alienated from their peer group, continue to look for acceptance in gangs and on the street.

Ewert and Wildhagen, citing Lochner and Moretti, write, "Increased educational attainment may reduce the likelihood of incarceration by raising the returns to work and so raising the opportunity costs of illegal behavior." However, the authors do not take into account the economic factor.[24] To students who grew up in poor, single-parent households wanting to emulate the rappers and basketball players on television or in advertisements, a high school education pales in comparison to the money to be made in the drug world. For many of these students, college is such a foreign concept that you might as well tell them that they need to travel to the moon. Yet even that reference may be too drastic; most of these at-risk students have never left their town, not to mention the state. They know that in reality, a high school diploma might qualify them for a job at a fast food restaurant flipping burgers, but they are never going to rise above their surroundings working minimum wage jobs. Educators and researchers preach that surrounding at-risk students with average or above-average peers will help them have higher aspirations, but the reality is that the social factors surrounding them are often just too great.

However, before we as educators can tackle the social problems that surround our students, we must first deal with the social isolation created in our schools when we label these students as students with special needs. With this label, we create a multitude of problems for our students with special needs. We generate social isolation for a group of students who already suffer from peer bonding issues. Our students believe that they are defective and need to receive special help to be on the same level as their colleagues. The stigma of special education tells them that they are not as smart as their cohort that haunts their hallways. Last, but not least, these students run a much higher risk of dropping out of school and ending up incarcerated.

However, we as educators can change all of this. There is not a one-size-fits-all formula that can be put in place to fix the special education system. What it will take is administrators and teachers who are willing to take a deep look at their practices and the system itself, and then ask the hard questions. What is causing African-American and Hispanic young men to be pushed into special education at such high rates? Why does the special education team resemble the inmate classification team? How can we change the isolation, desolation, and hopelessness that pervades the labeling of special education? What can we do to prevent young people from being incarcerated without receiving an education? Why do prisons and schools put their charges through the same testing, identifying, and labeling? Most importantly, how can I change this system for the better? The answers to all these questions lie within you.

NOTES

1. These names depend on the school district, but some names include *Intervention Assistance Team Meeting (IAT), Building Level Assistance Team meeting (BLAT),* or a *Teachers Assistance Team (TAT) meeting.*

2. Ohio Department of Education, "Whose IDEA is this?" Retrieved June 19, 2014, from: http://education.ohio.gov/Topics/Special-Education/Whose-IDEA-Is-This-A-Parent-s-Guide-to-the-Individ.

3. U.S. Department of Justice, Federal Bureau of Prisons, "Inmate Security Designation and Custody Classification," September 12, 2006, retrieved from: http://www.bop.gov/policy/progstat/5100_008.pdf.

4. Ibid.

5. Ibid.

6. Ibid.

7. Ibid.

8. Ibid.

9. Some of these special programs include Drug Abuse Program, Mental Health Program, Financial Reinstate Program, and other court-assigned programs. U.S. Department of Justice, 2006.

10. U.S. Department of Justice, *Inmate Security Designation and Custody Classification.*

11. Ibid.

12. University of Buffalo School of Public Health and Health Professions, "Special Education Laws," retrieved from http://atto.buffalo.edu/registered/ATBasics/Foundation/Laws/specialed.php#EHA1.

13. Ibid.

14. The new definition of *IDEA* also includes traumatic brain injuries and autism.

15. LRE is now defined as the classroom that the student would have been in if he or she did not have a disability.

16. University of Buffalo School of Public Health and Health Professions, "Special Education Laws."

17. D. Losen, and G. Orfield, *Racial inequality in special education* (Cambridge, MA: Harvard Education Press, 2002).

18. J. M. Patton, "The Disproportionate Representation of African Americans in Special Education: Looking Behind the Curtain for Understanding and Solutions," *The Journal of Special Education* 32, No. 25 (1998): 25–31.

19. Ibid.

20. Ibid.

21. A. Segal, *IDEA and the Juvenile Justice System: A Factsheet.* The National Evaluation and Technical Assistance Center for the Education of Children and Youth Who Are Neglected, Delinquent, or At-Risk, April 2011, retrieved from http://www.neglected-delinquent.org/idea-and-juvenile-justice-system-factsheet.

22. This number includes people in both jails and prisons, but not those under community supervision. L. E. Glaze and E. Parks, *Correctional Populations in the United States, 2011* (Washington, D.C.: U.S. Department of Justice, 2012).

23. C. W. Harlow, *Education and Correctional Populations* (Washington, D.C.: U.S. Department of Justice, 2003).

24. S. Ewert and T. Wildhagen, "Educational Characteristics of Prisoners: Data from the ACS," U.S. Census Bureau Housing and Household Economic Statistics Division, 2011, retrieved from https://www.census.gov/hhes/socdemo/education/data/acs/Ewert_Wildhagen_prisoner_education_4-6-11.doc.

FIVE

Space, Place, and the Power of the Box

Space is a crucial way that people define their boundaries. Institutions define their space externally and internally, and by default, these spaces affect those within the institution. The spaces that institutions make their wards occupy are crucial to understanding the effects that the institution has on the mental and physical status of the ward. These effects come in the form of barriers that can limit the future of institutional participants. To understand the role of space as a barrier, how spaces are defined must be explored.

Prisons are one of the oldest organized institutions within the United States and the world. In Europe, where prisons evolved from workhouses, chaos reigned.[1] Eighteenth-century jails were disorganized, crowded, and dirty, with simple bars that separated inmates from visitors.[2] In these original jails, giant rooms held both male and female criminals of all ages. Most of these criminals were debtors who were confined to ensure that their debt was paid.[3] These debtors were locked away in jails where they had to pay for their room and board with help from family and friends.[4] Rarely did debtors earn their freedom. Even with the help of family and friends, debts accrued at a much higher rate than most families were able to earn. These early prisons lacked structure and security. Their main goal was to keep inmates away from society. Early prisons and jails were mostly profit-making institutions.

The first formally constructed prisons in England were the bridewells, which were constructed in the late 1700s as a way to deal with the issues of homelessness and vagrancy.[5] Construction of the bridewells was as much for reform as punishment; the caretakers of the bridewells were employed to teach vagrants useful skills. When the bridewells failed to reform, vagrancy and more serious felonies were committed. England shipped their criminals from Europe to America and later Australia. As penal transportation became unpopular in Europe, old decommissioned war or sailing ships were used to hold inmates. Inside these leaky, wet, moldy ships, cells were built to house inmates while they performed hard labor in the port cities. Hulks were home to terrible conditions, constant wetness, heat in the summer, and cold in the winter. Human waste was rampant, and disease could decimate entire ships.

Once penal transportation to Australia was halted, attention turned to the conditions of prisons within Europe. Literature began to appear that bemoaned the plight of the debtor; the danger to the debtor's physical being and immortal soul became the concern of reformers. John Howard, a vocal critic of the prison practices of the time, strongly criticized the idleness, filth, and lack of rules present in bridewells and debtors' prisons. Howard pushed for a prison that focused on structure, religious reform, and hard work; he believed that this could be accomplished through architecture, classification of inmates, and formal guards. In 1792, the first prison built according to Howard's ideals was opened by his follower George Onesiphorus Paul; this prison created an atmosphere that excluded men from their friends and family, yet nurtured their spirits and bodies, while denying the luxuries that could be purchased in the outside world.[6] Ultimately, it was not the European style prison that would become popular, but the American style.

Today's modern prisons are sometimes referred to as *prison compounds* or *campuses,* which contain everything needed to sustain hundreds of people. From medical facilities to athletic fields, prisons are total institutions. Total institutions were defined by Erving Goffman as institutions where lines between work, play, and sleep do not exist.[7] Essentially, inmates live within a single space, the institution. These modern total institutions closely resemble high school or college campuses.

Keeping both of these institutions safe is a demanding job. Prisons categorize inmates based on their scores on different tests. These tests categorize inmates' dangerousness to staff, other inmates, and the community. Once inmates have received their designation, they are placed in an institution that is equipped to handle their level of dangerousness. For example, an inmate who is violent toward other inmates or prone to violence is housed in a segregation unit to limit his or her exposure to others. Safety measures are also in place to try to protect the prison from visitors.

Visitors must pass through metal detectors and are subject to searches at the discretion of the correctional officers. Prisons also demand a specific dress code for people who visit the prison. These measures attempt to limit contraband from being smuggled into the prison. Rules for visitors are also in place to provide uniformity and structure to inmate visits.[8]

School security measures have also increased in the last few years as a result of school shootings and other problems in K–12 schools. Many schools have installed metal detectors, x-ray screening machines, pat down procedures, zero-tolerance policies, security cameras, and school resource officers (police officers). Almost all schools have some form of zero-tolerance policies in place, as well as additional forms of security for visitors.

The entrances to prisons and schools provide another area of similarity. In both prisons and schools, visitors enter through a main office where they are required to sign in, wear identification, and then check out. In all prisons and some schools, guests are often checked for contraband, or things that are considered dangerous or violate institution policy. Also, by keeping a record of who has entered the prison or school, if an emergency should occur, staff know who to look for and where everyone should be located. In addition to the element of safety that these check-ins provide, this label also establishes who belongs within the institution and who does not.

Even though the Philadelphia prison model did not become the predominant model within the United States and the world, pieces of the structure became popular as a way to exert control. The central element of the Philadelphia model was the actual building structure. The prison was shaped like a wagon wheel; a central observation tower was placed in the middle and seven cellblocks or long hallways with individual cells extended from the center. This structure made it possible for one guard, placed in the central control room, to see down each hallway, effectively controlling the entire prison from one point with one person. Jeremy Bentham took this idea of control to a new extreme when he invented a type of prison called the *panopticon.* [9] The panopticon is a circular building with a circular guard tower inside. A single row of cells for the inmates lines the walls of the prisons and each cell contains a window. Guards are stationed inside the guard tower, and the design of the prison allows the guards to constantly monitor the inmates without their knowledge. The backlighting from the windows illuminates the inmates' every move, while keeping the gaze of the guards obscured.

Modern schools have used a form of this architecture to help maintain control. When one walks into a relatively new school, the hallways fan out from the main office, giving a clear view of the entire building from the central office location. These long hallways make it easier for office staff, as well as teachers in their individual rooms, to control what happens in the hallways. It allows for a clear view of the students as they approach and leave areas of supervision. Hallways within schools are designed for a specific purpose, with separate hallways designated for freshman, sophomores, juniors, and seniors that contain each group's classrooms and lockers. Sometimes even special education rooms have their own hallways, further separating students.

Returning to prison design, prisons use cellblocks as a way to house inmates by their classifications. For example, prisons have cellblocks that contain the mentally ill, dangerous inmates, new inmates, old inmates, sick inmates, gang-involved inmates, and others of varying designations. These cellblocks permit for ease of control by allowing movement and observation. In this way, cellblocks mirror school hallways.

Within the cellblocks in prisons are individual cells; these cells are where inmates spend most of their time (depending on their security level). The American Correctional Association requires that inmates who are held in single occupancy cells have thirty-five square feet of space; in cells with multiple inmates (*multiple* can mean anywhere from two to sixty-four), there must also be thirty-five square feet of space per inmate.[10] When an inmate is confined to the cell for more than ten hours a day, there must be eighty square feet of space.[11] The cell is the hub of the inmate's life. Similarly, the classroom is the center of the student's life.

To understand the development of the classroom, a bit about the history of modern schools needs to be discussed. The modern school as we know it formed in the cities around the early 1900s as immigrants poured into the United States from Eastern and Southern Europe. This mass exodus swelled cities on the eastern coast of the United States since immigrants stayed near these bustling port cities taking jobs as laborers and settling with others from their home countries. Most families put their children to work in factories because of their desperate need for money. However, with the passing of child labor laws, children became unemployable. Port cities were dirty, crowded, and overrun with children who would beg, steal, beat, or pickpocket from people on the streets.

As the conditions on the streets of major cities worsened, the cry for action became louder. City residents wanted the children off the streets so that the cities would be safer. The answer to this demand came in the form of mandatory attendance laws for school-age children. To make schools effective, changes would have to occur. First, schools would have to expand. Large buildings, similar to factories but with columns in front, were built to handle record numbers of children. Due to space issues in cities, this meant that these large buildings had multiple flights of stairs, poor lighting, inadequate ventilation, tiny windows, and other problems, similar to most buildings of the day. Once these schools were constructed, there was very little money left for upkeep.

The young women who chose to teach in these schools faced life-or-death situations. Classrooms were freezing cold in the winter and sweltering in the summer with water leaks, drafts, mold, and other issues that made teaching a health risk. Falling down flights of stairs was a real risk as teachers scurried up and down the stairs all day.[12] Additionally, classes were large; up to forty-five students were squeezed into one room.[13] Desk space was limited and many students made do with the space they could find. Books for each student were rare and most students shared books that had been passed down from generation to generation.

The focus of schools was not the actual learning of knowledge or content, but the Americanization of the immigrant child. Unlike the immigrants who had earlier come from Northern and Western Europe, who had proven themselves to be hard workers and adept at adapting to the American culture, the new Southern and Eastern Europeans were viewed as lazy and unwilling to change. This made Americans and other settled immigrants wary; their concerns stemmed from the fear of losing the American dream. As ethnic enclaves of Eastern and Southern Europeans emerged in cities, these fears increased. Society worried that the American values that they had worked so hard for would disappear with this massive influx of assimilation-resistant immigrants.

Schools were then forced to become the social institution that Americanized all youth. Schools became places where language, patriotism, morals, values, ethics, and other American traits were taught. Many boys did not graduate from school; they simply left when they spoke passable English and were old enough to hold a job. Girls stayed in school slightly longer than their male counterparts and were more likely to graduate; upon graduation girls hoped to secure a job or recommendation as a teacher or a nanny. If a girl left school early, she became a maid, seamstress, or cook, or took other types of low paying jobs, leaving her vulnerable to poverty. Even an education did not guarantee a better life; teaching was not a noble profession and teachers lived on the same poverty level as their students. [14]

Despite these issues, city schools were considered epicenters of learning. John Dewey used city schools for his grand experiments in learning, attempting to enhance learning for thousands of students. Other theorists used city schools to test their theories; these schools provided the perfect testing grounds. Thousands of students were available to researchers, allowing them to see the results of their experiments in everything from curriculum to discipline.

As time progressed, the more affluent in the cities began to migrate to spaces outside of the cities to escape. Wealthy movers demanded that the suburbs acquire all the luxuries that they had had in the cities. This included railroad lines, trolleys, electric, water, sewer, and other amenities. Convenience also came in the form of schools; wealthy parents wanted their children to attend better schools than were found in the cities. Parents wanted the innovation that was found in city schools, combined with the classic education of the elite. Soon, schools were created that combined the efficiency, innovation, and control of the city schools with the personalized learning of the classical education favored in Europe.

No matter where the school was located, for students, classrooms became their home away from home. As time passed and child labor laws were enforced with more vigor, seeing youth in schools became a norm. As schools learned to better balance their multiple roles in society, certain changes began to appear. Class sizes were narrowed as research showed that smaller classes provided better learning environments. Teachers began to receive more education and training, focusing on the actual aspect of teaching knowledge. Medicine improved, providing vaccines and better treatments for those exposed to diseases, especially teachers. Immigration from Europe slowed as the United States enforced immigration bans. Although cities remained crowded, the wealthier populations began to slowly expand toward the suburbs. Schools themselves began to transform, building control mechanisms that mirrored prisons into their schools that helped to ease the strain on teachers.

Classrooms began to resemble prisons cells. Today, students spend most of their day in classrooms, sitting in small desks, without the ability to leave unless permission has been granted. Attendance is taken in each classroom to make sure that students are accounted for and at their required location at the appropriate time. In some schools, overcrowding is an issue and this overcrowding can lead to problems with learning and safety.

A study conducted by C. Kenneth Tanner at the University of Georgia found that a classroom of ten high school students and one teacher needed 704 square feet total or 64 square feet per person.[15] For a classroom of twenty students and one teacher, 1,344 square feet is the minimum needed to provide an adequate learning environment.[16] The actual space available within most classrooms is actually much closer to the situations inmates find themselves faced with inside their cells. According to the Ohio School Facilities Report, classrooms are generally nine hundred square feet for one teacher and twenty-five students,[17] which amounts to a thirty-by-thirty foot square room. This means that the teacher and students have 34.6 square feet per person, or 0.4 square feet less than an inmate. According to calculations conducted using Tanner's table, twenty-five students, and one teacher should ideally be working in 1,696 square feet.[18] A 1,696 square foot room is approximately a forty one-by-forty one foot room, which means that the dimensions of an average sized classroom would need to be increased by eleven feet.

The situation is even more dire for students in special education. The Individuals with Disability Education Act requires that there be no more than twelve students with learning disabilities or sixteen cognitively delayed students in a 450-square-foot classroom, half the size of a regular classroom.[19] In this set up, students with learning disabilities are given 37.5 square feet per student, or a six-by-six foot space, and cognitively delayed students are given 28.1 square feet per student, or a five-by-five square foot space. Students are confined to rooms with dimensions similar to prisons and inmates for approximately seven hours a day.

Beyond the scope of the physical spaces and safety precautions in prisons and schools, each institution offers similar services to their wards. Since prisons are total institutions where inmates live, work, and sleep, the institution must provide most services for their inmates. Prisons are in charge of providing three or more meals a day that meet the nutritional recommendations from the government. Dental, vision, medical, mental health, drug counseling, and other services are provided for inmates.

If deficits are detected in speech or education or mental issues are suspected during the initial screening process when inmates enter prison, further skill acquisition and treatment will be provided by the prison. If the inmate has not obtained a high school education, the inmate will work toward obtaining a General Equivalency Diploma or a certification in a vocational program. Prisons also provide transition programs for inmates who will eventually be transitioning to the real world. Educational goals, along with transitional skills for the inmates, are often outlined as part of the sentencing procedures for inmates.

More recently, schools have had to offer these same services to their students. In addition to serving lunch to all students, schools sometimes provide breakfasts, dinners, and occasionally backpacks of food for the weekend to students who qualify. These meals are required to meet strict guidelines from the United States Department of Agriculture.[20] Mental health, vocational education, dental services, and work study services are also offered by schools to help provide treatment and assistance to students who are in need or do not fit into the standard educational mold. In a way, schools have become like total institutions in the care that they need to provide for their students. Schools are now responsible for the total health of their students.

By turning schools into total institutions that raise students in spaces that are confined, routine, and restricting, the students' creativity is stifled and they are taught to be comfortable within the metaphorical box. Therefore, when these same students end up either in prison or jail, their cells barely seem different than their classrooms. Scarier, however, is what this does to students' inquisitive nature and natural curiosity. Instead of brightening and expanding the horizons of the students, these prison-like classrooms make students fearful of the world beyond the classroom, since the world beyond the classroom is not static or as controlled as the world of schools.

For students who do manage to graduate and attend a four-year university, the effects of this incarceration in schools can be detrimental to their success. A good friend who teaches an introduction to education course at a major university has spoken many times about the worries that she has for the generations of students growing up in the No Child Left Behind era.

This year during her class, an introduction to teaching children's literature for education majors, a young lady was presenting on the book *Henry's Freedom Box*. In the story based on real life events, Henry mails himself in a large crate to the city of Philadelphia to escape slavery. As the young woman presented, she said, "Clearly, he [Henry] had to have someone else address his crate because he could not read or write." As silence descended from the woman's classmates, the teacher asked the young woman what made her believe that Henry could not read or write.

The young woman responded that it was not a belief, but that everyone knew no African-American people who were slaves could read or write. When the professor questioned the young woman about people like Nathaniel Turner, Fredrick Douglas, or W. E. B. Du Bois, the young woman had no idea; she did not know that they had existed and did not know their roles in shaping the future of this country. As the teacher explained the roles these educated men had played in the emancipation movement, as well as the fact that there were slaves who had been educated by their owners or by others, this young lady essentially shut down.

This young woman is not stupid. Her written work and participation in class had been excellent. For whatever reason, however, this young lady could barely function throughout the rest of that class. While part of this story can be seen as the failure of a school system to teach fundamental knowledge (or the young woman's failure to learn taught knowledge), it is possible that this is not a failure in teaching, but a failure of space. As new information was presented to this young lady, her mind, so used to being confined into the spaces allowed by public school, could not handle the new information she was being given, so she shut down.

The boxes that schools are putting students in are both metaphorical and real. These boxes are both physical and mental; students' minds are as confined as their bodies. New information scares most students. They want the routine, the comfortable, and the known. For students who go straight into the workforce, their encounters with knowledge that challenges their perception may be more limited than those who attend universities or colleges. That is not to say that they do not encounter new knowledge, but that the knowledge they encounter is less likely to be as shocking. For example, there are very few careers or jobs that would put workers into contact with *Henry's Freedom Box* directly out of high school.

College floods the formerly contained students with freedoms that they could never imagine: freedom of space (no longer confined by the bell system), freedom of thought, freedom of action, and most importantly, freedom of academics. Students have to decide on a major, pick their classes, choose to attend class, complete homework, and absorb the new knowledge being presented to them. In a transition period that is only a week (often referred to as *syllabus week* by the students), professors or teaching assistants lay out their expectations, the goals of the class, and what information will be covered.

After that brief overview, the tornado that is college for most students starts on the following Monday morning. Some students adjust perfectly fine; they enjoy the freedom. Most students panic, worry, and stress their way through college, knowing that they have to get through the pain to get the job they desire. These students often learn the information only for the test; taking in the new information, new experiences, and the new freedoms are too much for them to absorb all at once. They have to choose the one or two freedoms that they can handle, often choosing the physical freedoms and thought freedoms that come with the college experience. Academic freedom is something that they cannot handle; they want the routine, boxed-in spaces that their high school provided. Therefore, they learn the material enough to recite it for the test, to make the grade, and then they promptly forget the material as soon as the test is over. It serves no purpose in their lives, other than as a means to their chosen end.

This does not mean that students are shallow and self-serving. In an era where society is more connected to the world than ever before by the Internet and social media, change is a constant factor. For students attempting to form an identity in a chaotic world of fads, trends, and constant shifts, the knowledge that they attain is something that is theirs and they can claim it as uniquely their own. Since knowledge is formed by students making sense of the information that received from the outside world, the acquisition of knowledge is a deeply personal occasion. When this knowledge is attacked or questioned, through challenging academic freedoms, students may withdraw because they feel personally attacked. In the case of the young lady in the children's literature class, the knowledge that she had created—that no African-American slaves could read or write before emancipation—was part of the knowledge that she had personally created. When my friend introduced the concept of educated slaves to this young lady, the knowledge that she had formed through previous years of schooling was suddenly destroyed. This destruction of knowledge probably led to deeper questions that could make her fundamentally question the identity that she had formed.

Blame cannot be placed solely on these students for their avoidance of freedoms. Space defines us, creating the borders and boundaries that make us who we are in society. Most high school students feel powerless. Their schedules are determined by their educational tracks (do not believe the lies—there are still educational tracks), their parents, teachers, friends, future careers, and a host of other things that are out of their control. Once they accept that schedule and attend classes, the space in the classroom dominates their learning. Crammed into desks that sometimes border on too small, the space for each student is set. Each student is allotted his or her desk space, no more, no less, regardless of what the student's personal need for space may be. One student may need his or her desk space plus an extra inch on each side to feel comfortable, whereas another may need to have four feet of space around the desk. Classrooms rarely allow for this type of freedom.

Instead, the control is handed to the teacher through the confined space within the classroom. A brief story will illustrate how space within a school can feel confining and limiting. A local high school teacher was feared for her reputation as a tough English teacher. She demanded excellent and creative work from her students. Mrs. Kostraba[21] was a veteran teacher who struck fear into the hearts of her current high school students, but was revered by former high school students. Her influence on my future was immense and part of the reason for my chosen major in Secondary English Education. However, as a freshman taking her class and hearing the horror stories, entry into her class was tinged with major trepidation. That first day I chose a seat in the back corner, closest to the door. However, Mrs. Lynn was not letting us choose our own seats.

Pretty soon we were seated in alphabetical order by last name in rows. With my last name, my place was in the first seat in the second row and directly in front of me stood a painting of a guillotine. My memories of sitting in class that first day include morbidly thinking to myself that this was a signal that my head would soon be on that chopping block. Yet what made me most uncomfortable about that seat (you would think the guillotine would be enough, although soon a strange admiration for that painting developed) was sitting in the front row with five people behind me.

My height, almost six feet to be exact, is fairly tall for a woman, and freshman year of high school found me at approximately five feet eleven inches tall. That left me as the third tallest person in my freshman class and probably in the top ten list of the tallest people in the high school. For me, sitting in the front was excruciatingly painful. Ducking or slouching, especially while seated was my main mode of sitting; if I stuck my feet out, Mrs. Kostraba would trip on them. This was incredibly uncomfortable. Bent over my desk with my toes pushed up against the legs of my desk so that the temptation to stretch my legs out into my teacher's way was one way of coping with being uncomfortable. However, nothing was ever said that hinted at the lack of comfort I felt in the class.

Fortunately, my physical discomfort was put aside to learn, but others were not so fortunate. My brother is six foot nine inches tall and he has some horror stories about not fitting into desks, bumping his head on doorways, and tripping people because he did not fit into the confined space. Luckily for him, we share the ability to put aside physical discomfort and learn, but if we did not possess that trait, it would have been a very rough road for both of us. Space therefore is very person dependent; it varies according to the person, the action, and the time.

This feeling of discomfort is the focus of the concept of modern prison. Inmates were not to be made comfortable, hence the deplorable conditions of early places of confinement. The comfort of the inmate was not even taken into consideration. Prisons were designed to separate and confine. One group that has lobbied for more humane treatment of inmates and better living conditions has been the Pennsylvania Prison Society. This nonprofit group began in 1787 and throughout the years has advocated for those incarcerated and their families.[22] Many groups such as this exist in the United States and throughout the world, advocating for better conditions for inmates and their families. One of the ideas they encourage is the use of more space for inmates.

Prisons still use confinement and space as a punishment. Limiting convicts' freedom is one of the key parts of the punishment process in the United States. As humans, we crave contact with family, friends, and strangers, but we use space to create boundaries. In prison, forcing criminals to constantly share their space at all times is one freedom that is taken away. According to the current mentality, inmates do not deserve the freedom of space boundaries. Many inmates who serve significant amounts of time in prison or jail often find that readapting to the space boundaries issued by others is a difficult feat. This readjustment problem is similar to the one that college-bound students face. As members of a space-conscious society, we often adapt to other people's space boundaries without problems. As an observer, I often watch people react to space boundary issues and their reactions often surprise me.

Once, while in an airport tram, I watched a young woman with a large bag squeeze into a space that a pencil would have found tight. She was wearing headphones and quickly zoned out as the tram started moving to our next location. As I watched, the people that were being touched by the young woman and her bag became fidgety. A man in a business suit with a briefcase stood on one side of her, shooting her nasty glances as her bag repeatedly bumped his briefcase. Another woman on the other side clicked her nails against the pole, rolled her eyes, and sighed loudly, trying to signal her annoyance. A man in front of this young lady eyed her coldly as her bag bumped against his leg. The last woman that bordered this young lady actually tried to move away from the young lady, however, the train was very full and her movements only caused a chain reaction that had everyone glaring at everyone. In those moments (it only took about six minutes for us to reach our destination), I realized how important space is to us as society. From my position in the back corner, with the door and the corner of the tram as two of my barriers, when the doors opened, everyone on the tram breathed a collective sigh of relief. At least inside the larger building, space was available for us to stake out as our own.

Reflecting on that story reveals an inherent challenge. Notice space boundaries, your reactions to them, and how you erect boundaries. Within your classrooms, maybe the young man who fidgets in his assigned seat is not trying to be a pain; maybe he is merely uncomfortable with his confined space. The girl in the front row who seems distracted may be worried about how much space she takes up in the front row. These small indicators can hint at a larger problem; these students may be so used to their confined spaces that the future scares them. The question is then, with the space limitations placed on schools and teachers, how do we find ways to turn these confined spaces into wide-open spaces for students?

Beyond the idea of the metaphorical box that we educate our students in (whether deliberate or not) is how our institutions delineate themselves from the greater society. Razor wire, guard towers, double fences, and ground sensors are just one way prisons define their grounds from the communities where they are built. These measures are intimidating and send the message that evil people, unfit for human contact, are housed within. Security measures like these send a dual message; no one comes in, no one gets out. In a way, these measures make those of us on the outside feel secure, safe, and content; we see the barriers and we know we are protected.

Schools have a version of this same type of security, although much more subtle. Perimeters that surround schools are labeled with school zone signs, well-manicured lawns, and lights to give them a clean and well-kept look. This style sets schools apart from their neighborhoods, since most neighborhoods treat their schools as though they were places of reverence, trying to provide the best to the schools. Once a person enters school grounds, certain rules apply. Due to the Gun Free School Zone Act, anyone carrying any type of weapon onto school property can face significant charges or even jail time. Similar laws apply to people carrying illegal drugs, knowingly or unknowingly. Some states even have rules that prosecute certain crimes, like drug crimes, more seriously if the act was committed near a school.

A strict process controls entrance into both institutions. First, guests must enter through a series of doors that can be locked from within the main office. Once guests reach the main office, they are required to sign-in and show identification, often a driver's license. After signing in, guests are given some form of an identification mark or badge that marks them as a guest of the institution. Some schools and most prisons require that guests then go through metal detectors or body scanners to ensure that there is no illegal contraband entering the institution. When these steps are completed, guests are not allowed unrestricted access to the institution; there are designated places and spaces for guests. In the case of prisons, this process is supposed to be intimidating. It serves as both a warning and a safety feature. The process in schools is demanded because of security, but it can deter parents from being involved in their child's schooling.

Security measures can cause anxiety for parents who are unsure of the process, uncomfortable, have had bad experiences with school, or who are limited in their ability to speak the language fluently. Language is a major barrier to parents, family, and friends in visiting institutions like prisons or schools. Although schools are required to have translators when formal meetings are called, like parent-teacher conferences, Individualized Education Plan meetings, or disciplinary meetings, translators are not provided if a parent or guardian chooses to initiate a meeting. Budget cuts have also affected schools' ability to provide services like translators to parents. A friend who is a teacher in Denver related a story about issues at her school involving parent-teacher conferences and translators.

CeeCee has taught in a school district near Denver, Colorado, for several years. Currently, she has a class of nineteen seventh graders who speak twenty-two different languages. None of the students' first language is English and only one or two speak English as a second or third language. These students are all children of workers in the area and the parents themselves speak almost no English. The school is supposed to provide translators for the students' parents; however, budget cuts and the scarcity of translators has made this an almost impossible task. So instead CeeCee has learned a few tricks to facilitate the process. CeeCee herself speaks fluent Spanish and a few words of several other languages; however, she has found that the students themselves are the most helpful at translating for their parents.

In a chapter on space, place, and the power of a box, it is important that we examine both the physical and abstract boxes, powers, and spaces that encapsulate and define our institutions. These boundaries keep out those deemed undesirable and cause those who reside within the institution to be viewed with the institutional stigma, creating connotations, perceptions, and feelings about those within and outside the defined institution. These boundaries and assigned spaces let our students know who we believe they are, what their future holds, and how they deserve to be treated. What message are you sending?

NOTES

1. P. Spierenburg, "The Body and the State: Early Modern Europe," in *The Oxford History of the Prison: The Practice of Punishment in Western Society,* eds. N. Morris and D. J. Rotham, (Oxford, England: Oxford University Press, 1995).

2. R. McGowen, "Prison Reform in England, 1780–1865," in *The Oxford History of the Prison: The Practice of Punishment in Western Society.* eds. N. Morris and D. J. Rotham, (Oxford, England: Oxford University Press, 1995).

3. Ibid.

4. Ibid.

5. Ibid.

6. Ibid.

7. E. Goffman, *Asylums: Essays on the Social Situation of Mental Patients and Other Inmates,* (Garden City, NY: Anchor Books, 1961).

8. Federal Bureau of Prisons, "General Visiting Information," retrieved from http://www.bop.gov/inmates/visiting.jsp.

9. M. Foucault, *Discipline and Punish: The Birth of the Prison* (Paris, France: Editions Gallimard, 1975).

10. R. Miller, A. Thompson, R. Wener, S. Carter, D. Bogard, "ACA Guide for Adult Local Detention Facilities," National Institute of Justice, 1993, retrieved from https://www.google.com/url?sa=t&rct=j&q=&esrc=s&source=web&cd=3&cad=rja&uact=8&

ved=0CDEQFjAC&url=https percent3A percent2F percent2Fwww.aca.org per-
cent2Fstandards percent2Fpdfs per-
cent2FStandards_Committee_Meeting_August_2011.pdf&
ei=jwnfU_WWMajgsASd_4DICA&usg=AFQjCNGo-
4ukq0rHXvxwllsvwczMcenNmA&sig2=dBdSe_FPsj7upUbYVpxCeg&
bvm=bv.72197243,d.cWc

11. Name changed to protect privacy.

12. K. Rousmaniere, *City Teachers: Teaching and School Reform in Historical Perspective* (New York: Teachers College Press, 1997).

13. Ibid.

14. Ibid.

15. C. K. Tanner, "Minimum Classroom Size and Number of Students Per Classroom," 2009, retrieved from http://sdpl.coe.uga.edu/research/territoriality.html.

16. Ibid.

17. The Ohio School Facilities Commission, "Class Size Ratio," retrieved from ftp://ftp.osfc.ohio.gov/CM percent20FILES percent20& percent20FORMS/Policy_and_Procedure_Memorandum/Accelerated percent20Urban percent20(Big percent208) percent20Policy percent20Guideline percent20Documents/Class percent20Size percent20Ratio percent20_2-19-02_.pdf.

18. Tanner's table shows twenty students and a teacher would need 1,344 square feet; ten students would need 704 square feet. Five students would then require 704 square feet divided by two, equaling 352 square feet; 1,696 is determined by adding 1,344 square feet to 352 square feet.

19. Ohio Administrative Code, "Chapter 3301-51 Education of Students with Special Needs," retrieved from http://codes.ohio.gov/oac/3301-51.

20. United State Department of Agriculture: Food and Nutrition Service, "School Meals," retrieved from: http://www.fns.usda.gov/school-meals/child-nutrition-programs.

21. Permission given to use name.

22. Pennsylvania Prison Society, retrieved from http://www.prisonsociety.org/.

SIX

High School Clique or Prison Gang

Cliques and prison gangs are two social groups that have formed in each respective institution. These social groups wield tremendous power over those within the institution and can affect the way the institution runs. This chapter explores the formation of cliques and gangs, who joins and their reasons for joining, and the power exerted by these social groups.

The need for peer companionship begins at a young age; however, by age nine children are able to pick out the differences between each other.[1] Between the ages of ten and twelve, children begin to self-select into the peer groups of their choice.[2] In middle school, these groups become more pronounced and prominent, creating defined boundaries for their members. Cliques draw members with similar interests and traits; they use these characteristics to create boundaries between insiders and outsiders. These boundaries play a crucial role in the formation of cliques. Without outsiders, there are no insiders.

Cliques differ from normal groups of friends in several key ways. Unlike groups of friends, cliques have leaders who define the boundaries of the clique. Present clique members can be pushed out if they displease the leaders. Leaders may constantly exert pressure over the clique's members. Pressure can be subtle or obvious and cover a range of things. Girls in some cliques can face pressure over their appearance, which can lead to eating disorders, low self-esteem, bullying, and body image distortion. For boys, disordered eating is also a possibility, as is low self-esteem, bullying, pranks, drug use, or withdrawal from social interactions. Some cliques exert pressure for members to look a certain way or to dress a certain way; this can cause teens to pressure their families for designer clothes or even plastic surgery. To create the boundaries between those who are in the clique and those who are not, certain codes exist.

Boundaries exist to create safe spaces for those within the space to try and find themselves and their ideal identities.[3] These boundary lines can be either rigid or fluid, depending on the clique. For example, a clique composed of athletes would require that a new member be part of an athletic team; let us call that a *physical clique* since the members must be physically involved. For cliques that revolve around self-determined identity (i.e., the popular girls or guys, nerds, freaks, etc.), crossing the boundaries may be more challenging.

Some cliques form as a way for youth to explore and create identities. Other cliques form because of similar interests, but whatever the reason, cliques exist to fill the specific needs of preteens and teens. I have found, through the literature, that there seem to be three main types of cliques. These include the Identity Clique, the Physical Clique, and the Protective Clique. Preteens and teens look to their peers to figure out their roles and identities within their peer groups and to find acceptance. Every clique has a leader or leading group; think of cliques as concentric circles. The leaders of the clique exist within the smallest, tightest circle; the next circle is close friends of the leaders, which is followed by the friends of those friends and so on, until the farthest circle is reached. Depending on the clique, there can be many outer circles or just one.

These preteens and teens bond over similar interests but also for the support, sympathy, and protection that a clique offers. The old adage about protection in numbers is often what drives the formation of these cliques. When the popular cliques start to label those outside of their boundaries and treat them differently, those being picked on look to others in the same situation for understanding, protection, support, and safety. Protective cliques are a safe haven for their members; within the safety of the group the oddities that are fodder for bullying by outsiders are considered desirable qualities within the protective clique.

All cliques desire that their members adhere to certain actions, thoughts, behaviors, ideas, or beliefs that define the clique. Each clique's unique behavior patterns and ideals govern their treatment of those inside and outside of the clique's borders. Identity cliques have some of the most rigid behavior patterns and ideals, while protective cliques have the most fluid patterns. The strictness of identity cliques stems from the need to differentiate the borders of cliques. Dressing in the group style, using the same language, thinking similar thoughts, and fitting the image that the clique wants to present marks those within the clique.

Becoming a member of a clique can happen in several different ways. Some people actively seek to join cliques. This is especially true of popular identity cliques where membership is exclusive and elite. For different types of cliques, there are different admission processes. The leaders of the clique govern admission into identity cliques; therefore, leader approval is needed for new members to enter the group. For admission into physical cliques, new members have to become part of the group. This means joining the team or becoming a full-fledged member like in a fraternity or sorority. Membership in both identity and physical cliques is chosen by either the new member or a clique member, while protective clique admission is different. Other cliques often force membership in protective cliques through bullying, name-calling, or other fear tactics.

The boundaries that cliques create are delineated with symbols. These symbols are not definitive nor concrete. They can vary from clique to clique, city to city, state to state, and country to country. Identity cliques' status symbols often revolve around what is new, the latest trend, or the trend set by the clique leaders. Belonging to an identity clique can be an expensive undertaking; the newest trends in clothes, accessories, and technology come with hefty price tag.

Physical cliques use their activity as a boundary, but often there are other boundaries like clothing that designate a physical clique outside of the chosen activity. Athletic clothes from Nike, Adidas, or Reebok mark a member of a physical clique. Since protective cliques form to protect their members, they mask their unique identifiers. The nerd clique rarely goes around advertising their group by wearing dowdy clothes and talking in code.

While there are three main types of cliques, there are also significant differences in girls' and boys' cliques. Girl cliques are often identity cliques, built around a group of popular girls who become the leaders. The next level of girls in the clique are the best friends of the leaders. These girls are almost carbon copies of the leaders, except they lack the leaders' dominant personalities. Among the best friends there is constant maneuvering for the favors of the leaders; best friends will support anything that the leaders do. Sometimes identity cliques have third, fourth, and fifth circles or more; these members are distant friends of the leaders or the best friends. These distant friends must fit the image of the leaders, having the wealth to dress and accessorize in the style of the leaders.

The leaders that are glamorized for boys are members of physical cliques. Football players and basketball players are the most prominent. Therefore, in middle school and high school the boys considered most popular and cool are the athletes. These athletic boys are helped in their popularity journey by dating popular girls, just as pop culture movies and television portray. Like girl cliques, best friends surround the leaders of boy cliques, their best friends are members of the same team. Due to the team building activities that coaches use to create unity, teammates become friends off the field as well. Additionally, the amount of time spent doing athletics leads to friendships being limited to others in sports, often in the same sport.

The role of high school cliques seem simple: Cliques are either for popular, athletic, or other kids. But that is a very simplistic view. Cliques are a smaller replica of the social hierarchy that surrounds the school. Those who belong to the popular identity cliques often have parents who were popular during their high school years or who are currently popular in the community. Wealth is tied to popularity, especially in identity cliques and in some physical cliques, especially in schools where parents have to pay for their students to play sports. While wealth helps to create a hierarchy of cliques, most preteens and teens are already aware of their socioeconomic status.

All cliques have capital, most of it social capital. Cliques use this social capital to learn how to negotiate and vie for position and power within a social setting. As preteens and teens learn who and what are important to administrators and teachers, students take this knowledge back to their clique and use this knowledge to empower the clique. If students sense that athletics play an important role in the school, then physical cliques that center on athletics know that their capital is significant. If the school prides itself on its academics, then cliques like the nerds, geeks, and techies (technology gurus) have more powerful social capital. Sometimes these power shifts are not obvious and the power that cliques have can shift with school and community goals.

While cliques provide valuable social knowledge for teens, cliques can also have negative consequences. The external power of cliques has been discussed previously. Now it is time to examine the effects of cliques on those inside the clique. One of the negative aspects of cliques is the groupthink mentality. *Groupthink* is defined as a psychological phenomenon where the dominant ideas of the group cause individuals to lose their individuality and creativity. For example, when a group of individuals come together to brainstorm, a multitude of ideas will naturally emerge. When groupthink is present, instead of a multitude of ideas that arise, the group thinks similarly to one another and only a few ideas arise. Groupthink stifles creativity but groupthink can also lead to other negative actions and thoughts among the group. Issues like eating disorders, bullying, racism, and other problems can arise from the groupthink mentality in cliques.

Bullying has become one of the most prevalent problems in education today. School shootings, bomb threats, suicides, and countless other tragedies have been blamed on bullying. Unfortunately, bullying is a manifestation of groupthink and the need to create a boundary between those inside and outside of the clique. Bullying is defined as repetition of threatening, harassing or hurtful behaviors, actions and words enacted on either a group or individual by other groups or individuals.[4] Recently there have been attempts by various groups to stop bullying by leading antibullying campaigns in television ads. Teachers and administrators have attempted to stop bullying, but antibullying tactics have not stopped the issue of bullying.

Creating the boundary between those inside the clique and those outside the clique can be done through initiation rites. Initiation rites are sometimes referred to as *hazing rituals* and have negative connotations.

However, there is a huge difference between initiation rites and hazing rituals. Hazing rituals begin with the intent to cause harm to the inductee; the pain, humiliation, and fear are part of the intended consequences.[5] In initiation rites, the intent is not to cause harm to the inductee but to put the inductee through a process that will cause bonding with those within the clique. Almost every clique has some form of an initiation rite that they make their members go through; members bond over the shared experience of the rite, giving the clique a unifying experience.

Unfortunately, sometimes these initiation rituals cross the line and end up becoming hazing incidents. Normally, the initiation rites begin with the clique members who started the clique or have been in the clique the longest, as a test for the newest members to pass to show their loyalty. As new members pass the rites and become part of the clique, it is then their turn to pass the initiation rites on to new members. Sometimes it becomes a competition to see who can come up with the most unique or extreme initiation rites; when this happens, sometimes initiation rites turn into hazing rituals. One of the worst examples of hazing resulted in the death of drum major Robert Champion Junior at Florida A&M University.[6] The hazing ritual required that the inductee run down the aisle of the bus while other band members kicked, punched, and hit the new member. Unfortunately, the beating that Champion received was so severe that he died of blunt force trauma an hour later. Charges have been pressed in the case. As of March, 28, 2014, one ex-band member has been sentenced to a year in jail.[7]

Cliques will continue to exist and affect the social development of preteens and teens. Since cliques are part of the social growth process of preteens and teens, giving preteens and teens the tools to negotiate these tumultuous times needs to become a priority of both schools and parents. Even teaching preteens and teens about the techniques that cliques used to include and exclude members empowers them to understand and withstand the turbulent teenage years. Teaching children about their own self-worth at a young age can help them conquer the bullying that often accompanies cliques. For teachers and administrators, understanding the dynamics of cliques and the role that they play in the social growth of students is a key to helping students learn and cope with the outside, adult world.

Since cliques fluctuate rapidly, reflecting on my own experience with cliques would be outdated. It just so happens that I have a friend who has a teenage daughter who did not mind relating the social structure of her school to me. When I asked Nicole, a high school senior, about her experiences with cliques in her high school, her responses secretly pleased and worried me. It turns out, the same cliques exist now that existed during my time in high school, but their delineating lines, at least in this high school, are more fluid. I would like to add an interesting note here: Nicole's view and her friend's view (the friend happened to call during our conversation, so Nicole asked her) differed slightly on what cliques existed, the boundaries between cliques, and even the cliques that each young lady thought they belonged too.

There is a fine line between a clique and a gang; this line is normally drawn when criminal activity becomes part of the lifestyle. Multiple studies have been conducted that have tried to pinpoint the exact reason why preteens and teens join gangs.[8] Most of these studies have focused on boys, but recently studies have been looking at why girls join gangs. Boys have a tendency to join gangs for the money, prestige, and respect that comes with gang membership. Individuals' reasons for joining a gang are as diverse as the individuals in the gang, yet there do seem to be some uniting factors. One study found that boys with worsening behavior were more likely to enter gangs.[9] Young boys who show aggression are also at an increased risk for joining a gang.[10]

While worsening behavior and youth aggression tend to be male traits that signal possible gang interest, other factors put both boys and girls at risk for gang membership. Lack of parental supervision; coming from a disadvantaged neighborhood; a family member or close friend who belongs to a gang; or abuse, neglect, drug use, or alcohol addiction at home put both girls and boys at higher risk for becoming a gang member.[11] Coming from a lower socioeconomic neighborhood where disorganization, drug and alcohol use, abuse, social instability, unemployment, and a powerful gang presence can cause boys and girls to seek the familial and familiar comfort of a gang.[12]

Girls join gangs for reasons that are slightly different than boys and join at a much lower rate than boys.[13] However, in recent years, girl gang members have been on the rise. Girls who join gangs tend to be from lower socioeconomic neighborhoods, single-parent households, have seen drug and alcohol abuse, have been a victim or saw a family member be a victim of abuse, and lack parental supervision.[14] The gang becomes a substitute family for the youth.[15] Unlike boys, girls have two options for gang membership. All-girl gangs or all-women gangs are beginning to emerge as their own entities. In October 2013, the Bad Barbies, a subgroup of the all-woman gang, the Trinitarios, lost forty of their members to a federal and local raid.[16] Other all-women gangs include the Harlem Hiltons, the Hood Barbies, the Billion Dollar Beauties, the Gun Clappin Divas, the 2 Gurl Gunnas, the Blood Divas, and various others.[17]

Before the emergence of all-female gangs, male gang members used women and girls as sexual toys.[18] Females played a side role as arm candy, decoys, or baby mamas; female power depended on the male gang member who was currently offering protection. Women and girls had no power of their own and suffered abuse at the hands of male gang members. Initiations for these female members often involved rape by various gang members, beatings, and other abuse to prove their loyalty to the gang.[19] The draw was often the power, social structure, support, and family that came with the gang lifestyle.

For children who lack discipline and parental guidance, a gang may seem like a substitute for the family. Two types of gangs exist: organized gangs and disorganized gangs. Disorganized gangs are more fluid and bond together for the activity, then disperse or cling together loosely, until the next activity causes them to bond together. Organized gangs have rules, hierarchy, and structure; examples include the Crips, Bloods, Aryan Brotherhood, La Nuestra Familia, Latin Kings, Black Guerilla Family (BGF), Cosa Nostra, and Mara Salvatrucha (MS-13).[20] Depending on your location, there may be other gangs with more power.

Most present gangs are based on race; Aryan, Latino, African-American, and Chinese gangs have emerged as some of the most dangerous gangs operating within the United States and the world today. It is important to understand that gangs within the United States have a global reach; from Japan to Mexico, gangs of all races have made it to American soil.[21] In the 1800s the most prevalent and dangerous gangs in the United States consisted of White, Irish immigrants.

Today, the Federal Bureau of Investigation lists thirteen gangs as the most dangerous gangs in America. These are the 18th Street Gang, Florencia 13, Barrio Azteca, Juggalos, Latin Kings, Somali gangs, MS-13, Trinitarios, Pistoleros Latinos, Mexican Mafia, Mongols, Vagos, and Wheels of Soul.[22] Most of these gangs make their money running drugs and weapons, but their true danger is in their brutality. All of these gangs have members currently incarcerated, but for many of their members, prison does little to halt the violence.

Violence is a key hallmark of gangs. Their violence is directed at rival gangs and those who threaten their business dealings, but violence is also used against their own members. In order to join a gang, a new members are required to take part in a gang hazing ritual.[23] These rituals are drastic and dangerous; to successfully complete an initiation shows the gang that the new member is dedicated and loyal. These initiation rituals can include shooting, stabbing, harassment, taking a beating by older gang members, rape, sodomy, and a variety of other unpleasant ordeals. One of these rituals is called a "jump in,"[24] where three to four members beat the new member brutally. Once the beating is done, the members who did the beating pick the new member up and give them "love," and the new member is now a full gang member.[25] The idea is that the new member is willing to endure pain for the gang.

New gang members have to memorize the gang constitution and live by those rules.[26] For example, a notebook seized from an MS-13 member laid out rules that included avoiding certain colors, a pledge of silence, and various other policies.[27] Disobeying the constitution leads to the gang member being kicked out and becoming a target of the gang. Gangs can forcibly remove identifying marks, often tattoos, from the body of the person who is no longer in good standing. This is a gruesome process that can involve gang members holding down the out-of-favor gang member and burning or forcibly cutting the tattoo off.[28]

Gangs follow race lines, African-Americans join African-American gangs, Asians join Asian gangs, Whites join White gangs, Hispanics join Hispanic gangs and Latinos join Latino gangs. Race lines are not crossed.[29] In fact, some gangs like the Aryan Brotherhood are founded on their racist ideals. Like cliques, gangs have definitive and well-drawn boundary lines between those inside the gang and outside the gang. *Turf* is defined as the areas that are gang controlled; in cities, this is determined by blocks or certain streets.[30]

Gang members patrol the turf borders protecting their physical areas and people within the physical space from being attacked by rival gang members. Gangs follow racial boundaries. For example, if a Dominican gang enters Hispanic gang turf and kills a Hispanic member, the Dominican gang will go to the Hispanic turf and retaliate by killing one or more Hispanic members. The problem with this, besides the killing, is that those being killed are not always gang members. Nongang members are often caught up in gang violence simply because they live within the gang turf.[31]

While violence is an integral part of gangs, and the weapon of choice in recent years seems to be guns, some gangs pride themselves on their brutality.[32] Some motorcycle gangs and street gangs use stabbing as a way to send a message. Stabbing is a more personal form of assault or killing; in order to stab someone, the stabber must be close to the intended victim, making stabbing a more intimate act of violence.[33]

To stab someone also requires brute strength, especially if death is the intended outcome. Victims rarely stand still and they fight back, so the perpetrator must be physically stronger than his opponent to stab the victim. Rarely do gang members stab a victim once; even if death is not the intended outcome, most gangs have numbers that are considered sacred and they will often stab rival gangs members the sacred number of times, leaving a permanent impression of the gang attack on the body of the rival members.[34]

Violence is not the only problem associated with gangs. Most gangs deal drugs and participate in other illegal activities to provide financial support for the gang.[35] Few gangs allow free enterprise; free enterprise means that the gang members are able to keep their individual profits from their illegal activity. Most gangs function in a collectivist way; what gang members earn goes directly to the gang's financial officer (you may chuckle at this, but most organized gangs have a person or people responsible for collecting the money). From there, the money is divided with certain cuts or portions going to different members for other activities. For example, higher-ranking members receive more cash than the actual drug dealers, since the dealers are low on the gang hierarchy.

Gangs identify themselves through colors and these colors have ties back to the origins of the race that unites the gang. Starting in the 1970s and escalating in the 1990s, a massive gang war began between the Bloods and the Crips.[36] Bloods, a small offshoot of the larger Crips gang broke from the Crips during an internal gang war.[37] For the Bloods to survive as a gang, members bonded with small gangs and became incredibly violent. A gang war erupted between the Bloods, who identified themselves through the color red, and the Crips, who identified themselves through the color blue.[38] This gang war between the Bloods and the Crips became one of the most prolific and widely known gang wars in modern times.[39]

While the original idea of prison was isolation from family, friends, and comfortable society, these days, with the huge number of people in the United States incarcerated, prisons themselves often serve as micro communities. Since gang violence and illegal activities lead to incarceration, many of the prisons have become gang turf. In some cases, the prisons are actually run by the dominate gangs from the community. In Baltimore, Maryland, in April of 2013, thirteen correctional officers were indicted for smuggling drugs, cell phones, and for having sexual relations with Black Guerilla Family (BGF) gang members.[40] The BGF's gang leader impregnated several of the female correctional officers. In November of 2013, fourteen more correctional officers were indicted in the case.[41] Most correctional officers were recruited through family members, bribes, sexual relationships, or threats. Currently, all twenty-seven correctional officers involved in the case have been charged and have court dates scheduled.

The circumstances of the Baltimore case are not uncommon. Countless media stories have emerged in recent years about the prevalence of gang-run prisons or prison corruption cases. Gangs have flourished in prisons for almost the same reasons that cliques have flourished in high school. As gangs grew, more gang members were incarcerated; as these gang members were incarcerated, their numbers swelled and gang life continued inside the prison. Prisons are not isolated institutions; there is a vibrant trade of prohibited items that go on within prison walls. Correctional officers try to keep this in check, but it is not always possible.

One problem with gang incarceration is violence. Incarcerated gang members have plenty of free time, not a lot of space, and reputations that have to be upheld, which leads to inmate-on-inmate violence. Incarcerated gang members find each other, mimicking the gang structure on the outside world. Incarcerated gang members challenge the power of other gangs, harass new inmates without gang affiliations, follow orders issued from leaders, protect their prison turf by fighting, beating, shanking (stabbing someone with a knife made from materials found within the prison), or even killing other gang members inside prison walls. Often correctional officers are powerless to end the violence; they must control it in the best possible way. Even one gang member intent on killing another gang member wields tremendous power. Gang members can assist the perpetrator by engaging correctional officers in other emergencies or even physically fighting correctional officers to keep them from interfering with a gang fight.

Correctional officials have attempted to take a proactive stance on reducing gang power within the prison walls by sentencing gang members to different prisons and moving gang members around the country. However, this plan has backfired. By moving gang members around the country, gang-affiliated inmates have begun their own chapters in states where they never existed before. A prime example occurred when the Los Zetas, a band of former antidrug commandos trained by the Mexican government who became mercenaries for the Gulf Cartel, first made contact with the Texas Mexican Mafia prison gang to recruit new members to work for the cartel.[42] Los Zetas gang members are recruiting quickly and the gang is spreading through the southern United States. The gang is succeeding at establishing themselves as one of the most violent gangs within the U.S. borders. Other gangs like the Barrio Azteca, Florencia 13, 18th Street Gang, and Trinitarios have used their members to expand their scope and locations of operations.[43]

Drugs can be smuggled in by visitors or made inside the prison; shanks, knives and other stabbing utensils can be made through creativity and used with deadly force; cell phones smuggled inside can help gang members order kills, retribution, and intimidation of witnesses, and direct gang operations from inside the prison.[44] A simple pen can be made into a tattoo gun to tattoo members, marking their time in prison. New members can be recruited through the promise of protection, and skills can be honed as young, inexperienced gang members are put in contact with older, wiser gang members to learn how to be better in their activities.[45]

Gangs inside of prisons have been incredibly successful; many gangs even credit their starts to incarcerated individuals. These gangs are referred to as *prison gangs* because of their origins; the BGF, which began in San Quentin Prison, is one such gang. The Mexican Mafia gang was formed in a juvenile correctional facility.[46] Other gangs include street gangs, those formed on the streets for protection; most gangs are street gangs with origins that can be traced back to community protection. Examples of street gangs include the Bloods, Crips, MS-13 (founded in El Salvador), and the Latin Kings (founded in Chicago).[47] Regardless of the beginnings, once incarcerated, gangs can recruit new members who lack gang affiliations when they are sentenced to prison or jail.

Gangs are relatively fussy about whom they choose to enter their ranks. Not everyone is recruited or accepted. Just as cliques are choosy about who they let join, gangs also have member criteria. Besides the obvious passing of the gang initiation rituals, new gang members have to have traits or talents that are desirable to the gang. Young men and women who excel in physical violence, are easily provoked, and lack a close knit family unit are ideal targets for gangs.[48] Other young men and women who sell drugs well or perform other illegal activities well are sought after as new gang members.[49] Due to high rates of incarceration, new members are constantly needed to take the place of incarcerated or deceased members.

The desired criteria for new gang members differ from gang to gang, but members are selected with an idea of the role that new members will take on to help the gang become more prolific. Colors, as briefly discussed previously, are an important way for gang members to stake their claim on turf, people, and to display gang pride. As mentioned previously, Bloods claimed the color red for their accessories, such as hats or bandanas.[50] Crips wear blue or black or a combination of the two[51]; Latin Kings use black and gold beaded necklaces or rosaries[52]; and MS-13 tend to use blue or black bandanas around the wrist, neck, or forehead and athletic clothes that showcase the gangs favorite numbers, 13, 23, or 3.[53] In recent years, gangs have been more strategic about displaying their gang colors in an attempt to avoid detection by police.

Tattooing plays a prominent role in gang membership. Every gang has a tattoo insignia that is unique to that gang and is tattooed proudly and prominently on all gang members. MS-13 gang members use various tattoos to identify their members; most are large and prominent.[54] Sometimes older gang members have massive, prominent tattoos that affirm their status within the gang. The BGF's tattoos show a dragon wrapped around a prison tower, often clutching a prison guard and various weapons.[55] Crips use a six-pointed star and a crown within their tattoos[56] ; Latin Kings use a five point crown, the initials *LK*, or a lion.[57]

To mark turf, advertise power, brag about allegiance, or as a challenge to other gangs, graffiti is the communication of choice for gangs.[58] Graffiti is a language of unique signs and symbols that gang members have adopted; graffiti for each gang is distinctive and personalized. Rival gangs go into each other's turf and graffiti on buildings and other structures, attempting to assert dominance. Graffiti done in this manner is dangerous to all people within the turf, regardless of gang or nongang affiliation. Rival graffiti inside gang-controlled turf is considered disrespectful; such disrespect can start a gang war. There is a note of caution to be added here. Not all graffiti is gang related. In recent years, some people have made names for themselves with their graffiti work. These people have no gang affiliation and sign their work, or tag it. These non-affiliated graffiti artists go by the street name *taggers*.[59]

Most gangs are organized in a hierarchical manner; older gang members who are in good standing and have earned the gang's trust and have worked their way up the gang ladder hold higher positions with more power. Younger gang members with less experience and a shorter record of loyalty hold lower and less powerful positions. This is not a solid rule, but a good rule of thumb. Some gangs, like the BGF and MS-13 are modeled after a military hierarchy, even going so far as to name their leaders after military rankings like generals, majors, sergeants, and so on.[60] The MS-13 gang is especially dangerous and violent because many of their members have experience in guerilla warfare and training.[61]

Other gangs have loose organizational structures or community-based structures, which means that in one area the gang may look one way and in other area the gang looks completely different. However, despite their different organizations, these gangs are united under the overarching gang principles. The Latin Kings are a prime examples of this type of gang, as well as the Crips, the Bloods, the 18th Street Gang, the Outlaw Motorcycle Gang (OMG), and others.[62]

Gang chapters in specific cities are able to organize their gang to best fit the community, but gang members still live by the overarching principles of the gang. For example, the Hells Angels are a specific gang within the OMG; the Hells Angels have more than ninety-two chapters in twenty-seven states and are active in twenty-six countries all over the world.[63] In each area, the gang may be set up differently, but all gang members abide by the universal Hells Angels constitution. The Latin Kings are another example, and they pride themselves on their community-based organization.[64] Recruitment of new Latin King gang members takes place at church and during after-school programs as the gang views their constitution as their religion.[65]

So the question that should be asked now is whether it is possible to keep cliques from turning into gangs. The answer is not simple at all. There is no clear-cut way to keep a clique from turning into a gang. The sheer nature of a clique, by the boundaries created and members who are inside and outside the boundaries, automatically creates a power struggle and dichotomy that results in conflict. However, how schools manage this conflict can keep cliques from turning into gangs.

First, schools need to start taking back disciplinary power from police, resource officers, and other outside agencies within the school. Not every issue or problem within the school needs to result in the police becoming involved. Police involvement in schools put students in contact with the juvenile justice system for minor problems.[66] Juveniles normally placed within the juvenile justice system have serious problems; putting a student with minor issues in contact with a peer with major issues just does not make sense. Why take the possibility that those major issues will spread? Think about violence, gangs, and drugs as an illness like the flu. Putting students with a cold (students with minor infractions) in the same room with students who are really sick (think full gang member) almost guarantees that most of those with a cold will get the flu. Why, you ask? Because the students with the cold already have compromised immune systems and so their bodies are open to attack. Most students with minor problems, if handled inside the school, will never move beyond their minor issues, but if they are put in contact with really bad students, they will learn from them. A small problem that could have been handled in-house has just become a larger problem.

Second, schools have got to stop being punitive. How do we expect students to learn how to handle conflict and violence peaceably when all they see is exclusion and isolation? Think about this: When a student misbehaves in school, whether violently or not, what is our first reaction? Usually isolation and exclusion. "Throw that troublemaker out of school," "place him or her on suspension," "put him in detention," and "get him out of here" are the constant refrains.

No wonder some of these students think prison is a natural place. Troublemakers have been excluded constantly and taught that being isolated is the only place for them; good students are also taught that the only way to deal with those who break the law is to isolate and lock them out and away. What a sad world it is when isolation and abandonment are how schools deal with students who already feel abandoned, lost, alone, and isolated at home. It is little wonder that these left and locked-out students turn to gangs to find a family who will care about them.

All hope is not lost, however; some schools—especially schools in neighborhoods with lots of gangs and few other options—have turned to a model of restorative justice in their schools.[67] When a student commits a delinquent act, he or she is not only the perpetrator but also a victim. Therefore, the perpetrator, the victim, and others involved must come to a consensuses that is mutually beneficial for all involved. There is no throwing the perpetrator out of school or into detention because it is not productive for the perpetrator. In restorative justice–based discipline programs, one-way discipline policies do not exist. This is not an easy feat to achieve. As a society, most of us are punitive. If someone hurts us, we want swift justice and for that person to pay (literally or figuratively) for the harm they have done to us. Restorative justice does not work in that manner and for restorative justice to work, all parties, students, teachers, administrators, and parents have to believe in the system.

NOTES

1. New York University Child Study Center, "Social Life in Middle and High School: Dealing with Cliques and Bullies," *Child Study Center Letter* 10, No. 1, 2005, retrieved from http://www.aboutourkids.org/files/articles/sept_oct.pdf .

2. Ibid.

3. Ibid.

4. U.S. Department of Health and Human Services, "Bullying Definition," retrieved from http://www.stopbullying.gov/what-is-bullying/definition/.

5. Merriam-Webster Dictionary, "Hazing," retrieved from http://www.learnersdictionary.com/definition/hazing.

6. N. Hensley, "Ex-Florida A&M marching band member gets one-year sentence for hazing death," *New York Daily News,* March 28, 2014, retrieved from http://www.nydailynews.com/news/crime/ex-florida-m-band-member-year-jail-hazing-article-1.1738347.

7. Ibid.

8. J. L. St. Cyr, and S. H. Decker, "Girls, Guys, and Gangs: Convergence or Divergence in the Gendered Construction of Gangs and Groups, *Journal of Criminal Justice* 31, No. 5 (2003): 423–433.

9. B. B. Lahey, R. A. Gordon, R. Loeber, M. Stouthamer-Loeber, and D. P. Farrington, "Boys Who Join Gangs: A Prospective Study of Predictors of First Gang Entry," *Journal of Abnormal Child Psychology* 27, No. 4 (1999): 261–276.

10. Ibid.

11. K. E. Bell, "Gender and Gangs: A Quantitative Comparison," *Crime and Delinquency* 55, No. 3 (2009): 363–387.

12. "The Rise of Immigrant Gangs" (video), History.com, retrieved from http://www.history.com/shows/gangland/videos/the-rise-of-immigrant-gangs?m=5189719baf036&s=All&f=1&free=false.

13. B. Hamilton, "Rise of the Girl Gangs," *New York Post,* December 4, 2011, retrieved from http://nypost.com/2011/12/04/rise-of-the-girl-gangs/.

14. Bell, "Gender and Gangs."

15. "Turf" (video), History.com, retrieved from http://www.history.com/shows/gangland/videos/turf?m=5189719baf036&s=All&f=1&free=false.

16. http://fusion.net/justice/story/cops-bust-bad-barbies-female-gang-bronx-11206

17. http://fusion.net/justice/story/cops-bust-bad-barbies-female-gang-bronx-11206

18. Bell, "Gender and Gangs."

19. "Gang Initiation Rituals" (video), History.com, retrieved from http://www.history.com/shows/gangland/videos/gang-initiation-riuals?m=5189719baf036&s=All&f=1&free=false.

20. "Gang Library," HIDTA Gangs.org, retrieved from http://gangs.umd.edu/GangLibrary.aspx.

21. "Global Gangs" (video), History.com, retrieved from http://www.history.com/shows/gangland/videos/gangs-global-gangs?m=5189719baf036&s=All&f=1&free=false.

22. Ibid.

23. "Gang Initiation Rituals," History.com.

24. Ibid.

25. Ibid.

26. "Gang Constitutions Provide Order" (video), History.com, retrieved from http://www.history.com/shows/gangland/videos/gang-constitutions-provide-order?m=5189719baf036&s=All&f=1&free=false.

27. Ibid.

28. "Code of Violence" (video), History.com, retrieved from http://www.history.com/shows/gangland/videos/gangs-code-of-violence?m=5189719baf036&s=All&f=1&free=false.

29. "Divided" (video), History.com, retrieved from http://www.history.com/shows/gangland/videos/divided?m=5189719baf036&s=All&f=1&free=false.

30. "Turf," History.com.

31. "Code of Violence," History.com.

32. Ibid.

33. Ibid.

34. Ibid.

35. "Gangs and Drugs" (video), History.com, retrieved from http://www.history.com/shows/gangland/videos/gangs-drugs?m=5189719baf036&s=All&f=1&free=false.

36. "Crips," HIDTA Gangs.org, retrieved from http://gangs.umd.edu/Gangs/Crips.aspx.

37. "Bloods," HIDTA Gangs.org, retrieved from http://gangs.umd.edu/Gangs/Bloods.aspx.

38. "Crips," HIDTA Gangs.org.

39. "Top 10 Unsolved Crimes: Tupac Shakur and Notorious B.I.G.," *Time*, retrieved from http://content.time.com/time/specials/packages/article/0,28804,1867198_1867170_1867190,00.html.

40. M. Gray, "Racketeering, Smuggling, Sex with Guards: 25 Indicted in Massive Baltimore Prison Scandal," *Time*, April 24, 2013, retrieved from http://nation.time.com/2013/04/24/sex-with-guards-in-baltimore-prison-scandal/.

41. Gray, "Racketeering, Smuggling, Sex with Guards."

42. N. Rayman, "Mexico's Feared Narcos: A Brief History of the Zetas Drug Cartel," *Time*, July 16, 2013, http://world.time.com/2013/07/16/mexicos-feared-narcos-a-brief-history-of-the-zetas-drug-cartel/.

43. E. Goldschein and L. McKenna, "13 American Gangs That Are Keeping the FBI Up at Night," *Time*, January 15, 2012, http://www.businessinsider.com/dangerous-american-gangs-fbi-2011-11?op=1.

44. "The Rise of Immigrant Gangs" (videos), History.com, retrieved from http://www.history.com/shows/gangland/videos/the-rise-of-immigrant-gangs?m=5189719baf036&s=All&f=1&free=false.

45. Hutcherson, Donald T. (2012 June, 19) Crime Pays: The Connection Between Time in Prison and Future Criminal Earnings. *The Prison Journal* Doi: 10.1177/0032885512448607.

46. "Black Guerilla Family (BGF)," HIDTA Gangs.org, retrieved from http://gangs.umd.edu/Gangs/BLACKGUERILLAFAMILY.aspx; R. Valdemar, "History of the Mexican Mafia Prison Gang," *Police*, July 25, 2007, retrieved from http://www.policemag.com/blog/gangs/story/2007/07/history-of-the-mexican-mafia-prison-gang.aspx.

47. "Gang Library," HIDTA Gangs.org.

48. "Gangs Recruit New Members" (videos), History.com, retrieved http://www.history.com/shows/gangland/videos/gangs-recruit-new-members?m=5189719baf036&s=All&f=1&free=false.

49. Ibid.

50. "Bloods," HIDTA Gangs.org.

51. "Crips," HIDTA Gangs.org.

52. "Latin Kings," HIDTA Gangs.org, retrieved from http://gangs.umd.edu/Gangs/LatinKings.aspx.

53. "Mara Salvatrucha 13 (MS-13)," HIDTA Gangs.org, retrieved from http://gangs.umd.edu/Gangs/MS13.aspx.

54. Ibid.

55. "Black Guerilla Family (BGF)," HIDTA Gangs.org.

56. "Crips," HIDTA Gangs.org.

57. "Latin Kings," HIDTA Gangs.org.

58. "Gang Graffiti Marks Turf" (video), History.com, retrieved from http://www.history.com/shows/gangland/videos/gang-graffitti-marks-turf?m=5189719baf036&s=All&f=1&free=false#.

59. http://www.gangsorus.com/graffiti.html

60. "Gang Hierarchy" (video), History.com, retrieved from http://www.history.com/shows/gangland/videos/gang-hierarchy?m=5189719baf036&s=All&f=1&free=false.

61. "Mara Salvatrucha 13 (MS-13)," HIDTA Gangs.org.

62. "Gang Library," HIDTA Gangs.org.

63. "Hells Angels," HIDTA Gangs.org, retrieved from http://gangs.umd.edu/Gangs/HellsAngels.aspx.

64. "Latin Kings," HIDTA Gangs.org.

65. Ibid.

66. R. Casella, "Punishing Dangerousness through Preventive Detention: Illustrating the Institutional Link between School and Prison," *New Directions For Youth Development* 99, Fall (2003): 55–70.

67. J. Ashley, and K. Burke, "Implementing Restorative Justice," Illinois Criminal Justice Information Authority, retrieved fromhttp://www.icjia.state.il.us/public/pdf/ BARJ/SCHOOL percent20BARJ percent20GUIDEBOOOK.pdf.

SEVEN

Why Me?

Ethics, Ethical Leadership, and the Danger of Its Absence

Ethics: the definition can be elusive, vague, and unique. In fact, the best definition may be the famous quote by Supreme Court Justice Potter Stewart in the *Jacobellis v. Ohio* decision in 1964: "I know it when I see it."[1] While Justice Stewart was discussing pornography in his decision, a definition of ethics can be just as unclear, baffling, and mysterious as creating a clearly defined definition of pornography. Yet society demands that institutions and the people who work within them have an ethical code and lead from an ethically responsible position.

This leadership style, described as *ethical leadership,* does not come with set rules and guidelines. Instead, ethical leadership is decided on a *yes, no,* or *maybe* basis, based on the opinions, morals, and norms of those observing the institution or the person. In this chapter, ethics and their roles within politics, prisons, and schools are examined.

To begin the discussion about creating ethical leadership in education, we need to begin in a place that is far away from the school itself. Politics, the backbone of the country and of education, is the place where we need to begin the discussion about the creation of ethical leadership. As the United States has grown and become more diverse, the forces pushing for a say in the politics of the country have grown. Labor groups, single-issue groups, public interest groups, economic groups, and hundreds, maybe even thousands, of other groups have an interest in what goes on in the politics of the United States. Most of these groups are domestic, but it is not that simple; international groups are interested in what happens in America and they, too, hope to influence the decisions and policies made. The United States is not an island; our decisions and policies affect billions, both domestically and internationally.

89

Currently, we live in a society where people with money, lobbying groups, special interest groups, think tanks, corporations, and other large money groups influence the outcomes of elections and legislation. These financially affluent people and groups drive legislation that benefits themselves, their children, and their interests, protecting themselves from the others (i.e., poor) who would try to usurp the wealthy's position, given the least bit of encouragement. Whether this danger is real or perceived, the legislation enacted affects everyone.

States, special interest groups, lobbying organizations, and schools were upset about the No Child Left Behind (NCLB) legislation. The majority of states opposed the new legislation in a variety of ways, ranging from legislation or court cases. As states started to realize that NCLB was going to be implemented against their wishes, many searched for loopholes that would not penalize their schools. "Four-fifths of the states have sought waivers and exemptions from NCLB requirements,"[2] attempting to ward off the funding cuts that were going to hit the worst schools in the state. In 2011, Arne Duncan, the U.S. Secretary of Education warned America that 82 percent of schools would be labeled as failing.[3] Duncan's scare tactic missed its mark; however, some states did see adequate yearly progress (AYP) failure rates as high as 89 percent.[4]

The very premise that brought politicians together, to improve the education of at-risk and poor children, was the same premise that brought the special interest groups out in protest. Some of these groups included "the Children's Defense Fund (the creators of the slogan 'leave no child behind') [that] raised concerns about the overuse and misuse of tests,"[5] as well as "the National School Boards Association, the American Association of School Administrators, the National Education Association, and the National Conference of State Legislatures"[6]; most of these groups objected to the legislation based on the financial hardships that the states would face to fund the mandates of NCLB. As NCLB has persisted, schools have applied for federal waivers to the Obama administration, many opting out of the overly ambitious plans for universal competency of all students by 2014.

What no one dared to say about NCLB is its most important aspect. It was murmured in dark corners of schools, back rooms of universities, and sometimes out loud by those bold enough to take the backlash. NCLB came disguised in a package that gave the appearance of helping poor, minority, and at-risk students get on grade level with their more affluent peers. What everyone saw, but few could boldly say, is that if those schools did not perform superhuman acts of teaching, they would face sanctions, mostly fines, which would take away the already crucial funding that was so desperately needed in these schools.

NCLB was essentially a piece of legislation that rewarded high-performing schools for being high performing. As scores came back and slight improvements were seen, thousands of schools that did poorly on the testing were punished by the loss of crucial federal dollars. This could have gone on for years without a word being uttered; after all, poor schools and poor people do not rank high on legislators' radar screens.

In fact, this claim can be backed up by the 2013 Census Data. In the 2012 election, only 49.3 percent of people who had less than a ninth grade education were registered to vote.[7] Barely 50 percent (50.6 percent) of those who completed ninth to twelfth grade but had not graduated were registered to vote.[8] People who had a bachelor's degree and were registered to vote came in at 81.7 percent.[9] Women in all education categories were less likely to be registered to vote.[10]

Money plays an even larger role in who is registered to vote. Only 6.2 million people are registered to vote who make less than 10,000 to 14,999 dollars.[11] The largest group of registered voters make between 50,000 and 74,999 dollars and account for 20.6 million people.[12] Age plays a huge role in who is registered to vote; the older the individual, the more likely he or she is registered to vote.[13]

Being a registered voter does not automatically mean that the individual does vote; it simply means that paperwork was submitted. The group, Nonprofit Vote, found that only 62 percent of people who made less than 50,000 dollars voted, while 77 percent of those who made more than 75,000 dollars voted.[14] so it is little wonder that poor people have very little say in what legislation gets passed. So getting down into the dirty world of politics, why would legislators pass a bill that would benefit poor people, when there is very little benefit to their careers? As of right now, in politics there is very little incentive to lead from an ethical standpoint because no one else is doing it.

Let us examine NCLB, the sweeping school reform legislation that was supposed to create better accountability for all schools, set basic standards, and leave no child behind on the educational journey. This reauthorization of the Elementary and Secondary Education Act, passed by President George W. Bush, placed poor schools at a high risk of failure by demanding that students make AYP and pass basic state skill tests. If schools failed, NCLB financially punished schools that did not make these gains.

The poor urban and rural schools that failed to meet the demands of NCLB were not the schools that politicians' children attended; they were the schools of the unseen people. Politicians do not court urban minorities and rural voters, so their voices matter little to politicians and are rarely heard. NCLB did not affect wealthy suburban and urban schools. These wealthy schools were already performing at the top of the charts; their students were elite, coming from positions of privilege and power.

Outcry against NCLB was loud and vehement; however, NCLB was pushed ahead with gusto and vigor. Little documented research emerged about the dangers of this legislation. "Most of what we know about anti-NCLB sentiment comes from press coverage. Scant research has methodically examined the politics of NCLB or marshaled empirical evidence to investigate support and opposition to the act at the state level," declared Tom Loveless, the Director of the Brown Center on Education Policy.[15] Twelve years after the passing of NCLB, there are still angry rumblings from the press and powerful research conducted by university researchers that shows the detrimental effects of NCLB on poor, minority, and rural schools, but politicians have done little to change the burdens placed on these schools. However, one of the important things to remember about NCLB is that for the first time it required accountability in schools for all students (especially minority and special education students) and it linked these accountability tests to funding for the schools.

Meanwhile, NCLB still presides as the main educational agenda, even under President Obama. In March of 2010, Obama's administration sent the *Blueprint for Reform of the Elementary and Secondary Education Act* to Congress, which highlighted the problems created by NCLB and made recommendations for closing the gaps created.[16] However, no action has currently been taken on either the *Blueprint* or reauthorizing NCLB. In fact, the reauthorization of ESEA or NCLB is six years behind, with no solid plans for change.

Since Congress refused to act on either reauthorization or approving the *Blueprint*, the Obama administration has provided waivers for states for flexibility with NCLB. To qualify for a waiver, states must implement strong plans for career and college readiness programs, as well as "create comprehensive systems of teacher and principal development, evaluation and support that include factors beyond test scores, such as principal observation, peer review, student work, or parent and student feedback."[17] Currently, the only states without a waiver of any type are California,[18] Nebraska, North Dakota, and Colorado.[19] In March 2014, Washington State's waiver was revoked by Arne Duncan, Education Secretary, because the state did not link teacher evaluations to student achievement in a timely fashion.[20] Arizona, Kansas, and Oregon are also on high-risk status, meaning that without becoming compliant to their waivers quickly, their NCLB waivers can also be revoked.

President Obama's contribution to the realm of education has been his Race to the Top (RTT) initiative. This initiative encourages schools to generate better assessments and rigorous standards, implement improved data systems, create support system for teachers and school leaders, and increase resources for the lowest performing schools.[21] RTT has given over 4 billion dollars to nineteen states that have created plans for school reforms based on the four tenets of RTT. The nineteen states that have been recipients of the RTT monies serve 22 million students, employ 1.5 million teachers in 42,000 schools, and represent 42 percent of all low-income students in the nation.[22]

Recently, the focus has been moved from RTT and replaced by the Common Core State Standards Initiative. The Common Core State Standards Initiative was started in 2009 by state governors and commissioners of education as a way to create standards that used the best state standards that were already in place, the experiences of teachers, content experts, researchers, and feedback from the public.[23] Presently, forty-four states, four territories, the District of Columbia, and Department of Defense Education Activity have adopted the Common Core standards. Many of these new reforms have changed the way students are labeled, including drop outs.

While the national dropout rate has been shrinking in previous years, the overall rate was still at 7 percent in 2011.[24] Dropout rates in 2011 for White students went from 9 percent to 5, African-American students' dropout rates decreased from 13 percent to 7 percent, and the dropout rates for Hispanic students decreased from 32 percent to 14 percent.[25] American Indian/Alaska Native students comprised .7 percent of students in the 2010–2011 school year; their droupout in 2009 was at 7 percent.[26] Annually, this means that over a million students drop out of school, over eight thousand a day.[27] While dropout rates have appeared to be decreasing, changes in the way dropouts are identified may account for these decreases.

How is this ethical leadership? How can elected politicians say that they have the best interests of the public at heart when they continue to support legislation that dooms many of their constituents' children to prison or the streets? Yet politicians' children continue to receive education that is so far beyond the norm that they might as well be attending private preparatory schools. Why and how does this happen? Why do we stand for it? What would happen if politicians' children had to attend the same schools as poor urban or rural students? Would NCLB still be the answer to school problems within the United States?

School leadership does not a get a free pass in this conversation about building ethical leadership. Some schools allow failure to happen or push students either through or out to meet the AYP goals that keep them from facing financial restrictions or government takeover. It is not just advancement or failure that schools use to keep students moving. African-American and Latino males are often pushed into special education classes along with students who have behavioral problems because special education gets these problematic students out of regular classrooms, decreasing disruptions for normal students. Students labeled *special education* fall under a special category nominally affecting the AYP of the school. Several schools have been caught cheating on the testing, including schools in Georgia, Texas, Alabama, California, Washington, D.C., Maryland, Pennsylvania, New Jersey, Connecticut, Ohio, and others.

Schools, the backbone of the nation, where all children go to be molded into productive and educated citizens, are pushing out, labeling, failing, and cheating the very children that they are put in charge of to meet the standards set by the government. What happens to the students who cannot rise above the murky waters to graduate? Most often, these students drop out (at the conscious or unconscious urging of the school), commit crimes, and end up in prison. This simple cycle is being repeated as schools push to meet NCLB requirements or risk financial cutbacks or state takeover.

The emergence of widespread scandals and rumors of corruption in connection with the NCLB legislation is just one place to start. As NCLB took effect, the major ruckus being raised came from states that were fighting to not implement the new measures. However, as NCLB became an indomitable educational force, the testing aspect of NCLB came into effect. As schools implemented testing for all of their students, test scores became a pivotal factor in the funding that schools received. Since NCLB set higher and higher AYP goals for schools, test scores became crucial, especially for at-risk students. Scandals related to the politics of testing have touched numerous cities, including schools that were once touted for their incredible educational gains.

In an article in the *Washington Post* by Lyndsey Layton called "GAO: 40 States Have Suspected Cheating on K-12 Tests" published in 2013, Layton writes, "33 [states] confirmed at least one instance of cheating, and 32 states canceled or invalidated test results from individual students, schools or districts as a result of either suspected or confirmed cheating."[28] Some of these examples include New York, Atlanta, El Paso, Birmingham, Los Angeles, and many others; some have faced harsh penalties like jail time (Atlanta), while others have escaped with slaps on the wrist (New York).

No matter what state or what city the cheating scandals have taken place in, the one factor that has remained similar in all the cases is that the schools that have cheated have been worried about losing funding under the NCLB policy. In the wake of the Atlanta cheating scandal, a prominent member of the community was quoted by *USA Today* as saying, "If you look at Clayton County, Dekalb County, Atlanta, these are overwhelmingly majority African-American school districts. This is not about the children. This is about money."[29]

The Atlanta school scandal came as a surprise to many: "During the decade she [Beverly Hall] led the district of 52,000 children, many of them poor and African-American, Atlanta students often outperformed wealthier suburban districts on state tests. Those test scores brought her fame—in 2009, the American Association of School Administrators named her superintendent of the year. . . . And fortune—she earned more than 500,000 dollars in performance bonuses while superintendent."[30] The former 2009 national superintendent of the year, Hall now finds herself "charged with racketeering, theft, influencing witnesses, conspiracy and making false statements. Prosecutors recommended a 7.5 million dollar bond for her; she could face up to 45 years in prison."[31]

Hall, however, is not the first superintendent to face time in jail for a cheating scandal. Lorenzo Garcia, the former superintendent of El Paso, Texas, schools was sentenced to three and a half years in prison and a fine of $2.5 million.[32] Garcia's plan was similar to Hall's: bring improved test scores to his schools and get more funding. He wanted to improve test scores "at Bowie High school by not testing the poorest performing 10th graders, changing failing grades to passing grades and forcing struggling students to drop out of school altogether. It worked. Bowie's rating quickly went from 'failing' to 'academically acceptable.' Everybody looked great—the district, the school board, the state—while Garcia collected more than $56,000 in bonuses. He was nominated for Texas superintendent of the year twice."[33] Countless students were pushed out, ignored, or dropped out because of Garcia's policies for handling students that would not help his district's test scores.

These are only two detailed examples of schools that have been caught attempting to cheat the politics of education. The blame does not fall only on these particular schools. The president and Congress were warned numerous times by states and special interest groups that NCLB would present a huge challenge to poor, large, minority-heavy schools. These schools were often struggling before NCLB, but with the passage of NCLB these struggling schools risked losing crucial funding because of their test scores. The pressure to perform was on and unfortunately, the motto for some schools became success at any cost.

When schools fail, students fail, and this failure often leads these left-behind students susceptible to the lure of the criminal world. According to the National Dropout Prevention Center/Network at Clemson University, "82 percent of prisoners in America are high school dropouts,"[34] meaning that most students who are pushed out or drop out end up in prison. Once locked inside these institutions for whatever violation they have committed, society assumes that they will learn their lesson and be released as better members of society.

The last institution in this conversation is the institution of prison, which receives the fallout from both government and school failures. The perceptions of prisons, or locking away people who commit crimes, make those who are law-abiding citizens feel safe. Because of this feeling of safety, prisons continue to flourish. Prisons offer little in the way of rehabilitation to the men and women within the prison system. Education within prisons is subpar. Most inmates only complete a general education diploma (GED) and few can read or write beyond a seventh grade level. Drugs, gangs, prostitution, and other issues run rampant in prisons, offering little in the way of rehabilitation for the men and women within the prison. There is very little emphasis on psychological counseling, job counseling, drug rehabilitation, diagnosing of learning disorders, education, or even transitioning to the outside world. Inmates are viewed as chattel, stripped of their voting rights and caged, to perpetuate the feeling of safety required by society.

Most inmates have learning disabilities, mental illnesses, grew up in poverty, were victims of abuse, and are addicted to drugs or alcohol. Behavioral problems caused by learning disabilities are the number one reason inmates cited for dropping out of school.[35] College, for many, is an achievement that is on par with flying to the moon. Drug offenses, robbery, and gang violence are the number one reason for their incarceration. Certain states have passed legislation called "Three Strikes" laws; inmates who have committed three crimes are eligible for life in prison, no matter the severity of their third crime.

Prisons have not been without scandals; inmates have coerced guards into running drugs, committing murders, prostitution, and numerous other offenses that have made headlines in mainstream media. Baltimore City Corrections was recently hit with a scandal where guards were accused of smuggling, racketeering, and running a prostitution ring in conjunction with inmates. Issues of corruption in Ohio, Pennsylvania, Florida, Georgia, Arizona, Texas, Colorado, and other states have shown that even the institutions in charge of keeping society safe are not immune to unethical dealings.

Yet recent prison scandals involving both guards and inmates bring to light the fact that no place is safe from corruption. In 2006, Florida's Department of Corrections, which is the third largest prison system in the United States (128 plus facilities that houses 85,000 inmates) found themselves in the middle of a huge scandal that involved corruption, cronyism, drug rings, theft, brawling and misuse of inmate labor.[36] Corrections officers were accused of brawling among themselves at a banquet, placing inmates in no-show jobs, and treating inmates brutally.

In one case, says McAndrew, a former guard at one of the prisons who keeps informed about prison happenings through emails with current and past employees, "One warden took his prison softball team to Las Vegas, gave them $35,000 and said 'Have a good time, boys. You've earned it.'"[37] Governor Jeb Bush took action in February of 2006, attempting to clean out the staff of the Florida Department of Corrections and to improve the reputation of the prisons.

In August of 2012, the Federal Bureau of Investigation arrested a kitchen supervisor in a prison in Arizona for supplying inmates with contraband in exchange for sex.[38] Certain things within the prison culture are hard to obtain, cigarettes being one item that can earn an inmate profit. The kitchen supervisor would "give [the prisoner, 'E.D.'] a pack of cigarettes every two weeks. 'E.D.' would turn about and [sell] off the cigarettes to other inmates, netting as much as $150."[39] When issues like this come to light within the prison system, the deprivation that is supposed to be part of the process of incarceration is shattered, making the idea of prison somewhat moot.

Arizona is not the only state that has faced issues with inmate and guard sex scandals. The website Prison Legal News (PLN) lists multiple cases that have happened in Arizona, Arkansas, California, Colorado, Connecticut, Florida, Georgia, Hawaii, Idaho, Illinois, Indiana, Iowa, Kansas, Kentucky, Louisiana, Maine, Massachusetts, Michigan, Mississippi, Montana, Nebraska, Nevada, New Hampshire, New Jersey, New Mexico, New York, North Carolina, Ohio, Oklahoma, Oregon, Pennsylvania, South Carolina, Tennessee, Texas, Utah, Virginia, Washington, West Virginia, and Wisconsin.[40] Contrary to popular opinion, not all cases involve male guards. In the list on PLN, an equal number of cases involve women guards.

Most recently in April of 2013, the Baltimore city corrections system was involved in a massive scandal that shook the foundations of the idea of incarceration. Federal law enforcement officers say that from approximately 2009 until April 2013, guards "conspired with or took bribes from members of the Black Guerilla Family to smuggle drugs, cell phones, and other contraband in and out of the Baltimore City Detention Center. . . . Four female corrections officers named in the indictment even allegedly became pregnant by the gang's accused ringleader."[41] Essentially, the accused ringleader, who was placed in the detention center while awaiting trial for attempted murder, continued to run his gang, recruiting guards to help. It is speculated that the ringleader even ordered a few assassination attempts and knifings while in the detention center, using the phone.[42]

Too often, however, in the discussion of ethical leadership, the conversation simply focuses on the organization in question, never looking beyond it. It is a troubling phenomenon because in today's world, everything and everyone is connected. As catalysts of change, we cannot discuss making school leadership more ethical without looking at the other factors that play into education. No longer can we be self-contained; education is influenced and influences other institutions. It is no longer enough to say that we have to have change within schools; we have to change it all.

As leaders, we cannot hope to change one system without changing the other systems that feed into ours; and as much as we dislike the idea of prisons and politics working simultaneously with education, we need to face the reality that they are as important or more important than schools. To start building ethical leadership, we must first build ethical leaders. Ethical leadership sets the tone for the organization; ethical organizations are not perfect, but they attempt to do the least amount of harm possible.

The idea of building ethical leadership needs to start within the education system, but also simultaneously in other realms of society. If we truly believe that schools educate the future leaders of tomorrow, then beginning in schools is logical. However, beginning in schools is a slow place to start. It takes approximately thirty years for a successful change in ethics to take place. Even that plan demands specific things; throughout the hustle, bustle, and shady dealings of the world, the former student must be able to succeed while maintaining adherence to his ethical code. In a world where getting ahead often requires occasional moments of dubious ethics, this scenario seems terribly slow and fraught with peril.

However, if prisons, schools, and politics could work together to create a better society, laws and regulations could be created that were fair and just for all, especially in the realm of education legislation. This legislation would include fair and equal funding for all schools; in fact, it might even provide more money for poor and minority schools. Money is important; it hires good teachers, pays for new technology, keeps facilities up-to-date, and makes education easier for all involved.

The U.S. government has the ability to make funding equal for all schools in the U.S., but in a prior Supreme Court case, it has refused.[43] In education, if schools were funded equally and could provide every student with a worthwhile, relevant, and useful education, the possibilities would be endless. From creating an economic upturn to lower crime rates, education is a way to make anything possible. Also, if prisons were places that provided true rehabilitation for inmates and inmates could leave prisons and jails drug free; GED certified; and armed with coping strategies, medicine, housing, networks, and a host of other aids, recidivism rates would plummet and society would become safer.

Just as we cannot hope to see these organizational changes in a snap of the fingers, building ethical leadership will be a slow process. While there is a hope that creating youth with strong moral and ethical reasoning platforms could change all organizations, that is naïve. Corruption is rampant, and sometimes the lure is much stronger than even the strongest moral platform. As we are creating more moral students, we also need to be insisting on an overhaul of each organization. Let us take money out of politics; what could be possible if the best candidate could win, rather than the candidate with the most money? What would happen if prisons were run on fair and ethical treatment, looking to correct and help deviants instead of punish them? What if all schools were funded equally, deeply cared for, and did not let a student graduate without actually knowing the information? Would this help? Could it be possible?

I do not have the best answers. I do not even have good answers for how we go about fixing the issue of ethical leadership in education or elsewhere in the world. What I do know is that we cannot continue down the path that we are currently on. The corporate world, the political world, the prison world, and the education world are all tied together and so far, none have been without their issues. Building ethical leadership is going to take more than just a day, month, or year; building ethical leadership is going to take years.

The problem is that we have not yet started this building process. The U.S. government and schools are too concerned with mathematics, science, reading, and writing; we barely have time to teach those subjects before students are tested. How can we possibly have time to teach moral and ethical reasoning to youth? And if schools do not teach it, where will youth learn it? This conversation about ethical leadership needs to expand beyond the realm of education and collaborate with other organizations. Therefore, the challenge for you is to go out and start a conversation with whomever will listen, from whatever organization, about ethical leadership. Sometimes the hardest part of change is acknowledging that we are not perfect.

Let me leave you with a true story about the repercussions of letting things continue the way they are, without change. During a visit to a prison in Pennsylvania, I had an opportunity to speak with an inmate who is incarnated for life and he told me his story. Al[44] grew up in South Philadelphia, a rough section of the city, to a drug-addicted mother and without a male role model. As the oldest of four boys, Al felt that he had to become the man of the family and provide a living for his younger siblings. At age ten, his mother's then-boyfriend recruited Al to work as a lookout during drug deals in his neighborhood. By age fifteen, Al was dealing drugs, and at age seventeen, he joined a gang to make more money by getting access to more drugs through the gang. As part of the gang initiation process, Al was required to shoot a rival gang member. One night, Al and several gang members entered rival gang territory, intent on completing Al's initiation.

By this point, Al had completely dropped out of school. By his own admission, he could barely read and hardly write a complete sentence, but possessed strong math skills due to his street job. He admitted to me that life at home was so bad that he rarely spent time there, dropping off his earnings to his mother so that she could buy drugs and smuggling his brothers a small amount of cash so that they could buy food for themselves. That night, in front of his gang family, Al shot and killed a 19-year-old rival gang member. During this shooting, Al and his gang made one error: Al shot the rival gang member in front of a convenience store equipped with cameras. Twenty-four hours later, Philadelphia police located Al at a friend's house and arrested him for murder.

Al's young public defender, fresh from law school, was no match for the defense attorney. Six days after his eighteenth birthday, Al was sentenced to life in prison with no possibility of parole. After spending the first eleven years of his incarceration causing trouble, fighting, and denying his responsibility in his actions, Al told me he made a powerful decision.

He made the difficult decision to reach out to the parents of the young man he had killed and ask for their forgiveness. In what he described as the hardest moment of his life, he told me that the young man's parents had journeyed to his prison to meet with him in person. He told me that sitting across the table from the young man's parents, explaining why he had targeted and then killed their child was the hardest moment he had ever had. I listened to him describe how the young man's mother cried and the father just sat there with a shocked looked on his face, and how the experience made him realize that magnitude of what he had taken from their family.

Al told me that, at the age of twenty-nine when that meeting took place, he finally realized the gravity of his choice. When I spoke with Al, he was forty-five years old, he had renounced his gang affiliation, and earned his GED as well as certifications in heating, ventilation, and air conditioning; electricity; welding; mechanics; and other programs offered by the prisons he resided in. He had stopped fighting and become a model inmate, even being relocated from a maximum-security prison to a medium-security prison camp. Al had even appealed to the Governor for release request and the deceased young man's parents had written the Governor a letter in support of Al's release. However, the Governor denied Al's request for release. As of this writing, Al will die in prison.

I asked Al a hypothetical question: If he could change anything, what would it be? Without missing a beat, Al looked me directly in the eye and told me he would have stayed in school. When I asked him if he was just telling me this because of my background, he told me no. In hindsight, examined during countless hours of sitting idly behind bars thinking about his life, he realized that his math skills could have landed him a job as an accountant or even a math teacher. However, he admits, his bravado, ignorance, and cockiness at age sixteen had him believing that school was a worthless endeavor. With hindsight, he realized that because he struggled in so many key areas of school, dropping out was the easy way out. Al's lessons were learned the hard way and his dreams of being a spokesman to combat further violence will unfortunately die with him in prison.

How many other rehabilitated inmates will face the same fate as Al? Do we not keep our word? If we fail so spectacularly at seeing the Al's in our institutions, those that have met or exceeded the institution's goals, and yet we refuse to honor our end of the bargain, where are our ethics? Have we created institutions that uphold the ethics they are created on or do they simply pay lip service to a standard of ethics that we value? What does this say about our ethics and ability to lead in an ethical manner? Are our ethics real and solid or just a smoke-and-mirrors funhouse trick? Do we really know it when we see it or have we relegated our ethical leadership to the same place as our pornography, stashed in the deep, dark recesses of our closet?

NOTES

1. Jacobellis v. Ohio, 378 US 184. Argued March 26, 1963; decided June 22, 1964.

2. The National Center for Fair and Open Testing, "NCLB Opposition Grows, Work Remains," retrieved from http://www.fairtest.org/nclb-opposition-grows-work-remains.

3. Editorial Projects in Education Research Center, "Issues A-Z: No Child Left Behind," *Education Week,* September 19, 2011, retrieved from http://www.edweek.org/ew/issues/no-child-left-behind/.

4. M. McNeil, "Are 82 percent of Schools 'Failing' Under NCLB as Duncan Warned?" *Education Week,* August 3, 2011, retrieved from http://blogs.edweek.org/edweek/campaign-k-12/2011/08/are_82_of_schools_failing_unde.html.

5. Neill, 2003.

6. U.S. Department of Education: New York State Archives, "Federal Education Policy and the States, 1945–2009: The George H. W. Bush Years: America 2000 Proposed," *States' Impact on Federal Education Policy,* retrieved from http://www.archives.nysed.gov/edpolicy/research/res_essay_bush_ghw_amer2000.shtml.

7. United States Census Bureau, "Table 5: Voting and Registration in the Election of November 2012—Detailed Tables," retrieved May 8, 2013, from https://www.census.gov/hhes/www/socdemo/voting/publications/p20/2012/tables.html.

8. Ibid.

9. Ibid.

10. Ibid.

11. Ibid.

12. Ibid.

13. Ibid.

14. Nonprofit Vote. (2012). America Goes to the Polls: Voter Participation Gaps in the 2012 Presidential Election. http:nonprofitvote.org/documents/2013/09/america-goes-to-thepolls-2012-voter-participation-gaps-in-the-2012-presidential-election.pdf.

15. T. Loveless, "The Peculiar Politics of No Child Left Behind," *Brookings,* August 2006, retrieved from http://www.brookings.edu/research/papers/2006/08/k12education-loveless.

16. "Education: Knowledge and Skills for the Jobs of the Future: Reforming No Child Left Behind," *Whitehouse.gov,* retrieved from http://www.whitehouse.gov/issues/education/k-12/reforming-no-child-left-behind.

17. Ibid.

18. California CORE districts have been granted a waiver, not all California school districts.

19. M. McNeil, C. C. Hung, D. Nhan, and L. Williams, "NCLB Waivers: A State-by-State Breakdown," *Education Week,* March 20, 2013, retrieved from http://www.edweek.org/ew/section/infographics/nclbwaivers.html.

20. C. Emma, "Duncan Yanks NCLB Waiver from Washington State," *Politico,* April 24, 2014, retrieved from http://www.politico.com/story/2014/04/washington-state-nclb-waiver-arne-duncan-105997.html.

21. "Education: Knowledge and Skills for the Jobs of the Future: Race to the Top," Whitehouse.gov, retrieved from http://www.whitehouse.gov/issues/education/k-12/race-to-the-top.

22. Ibid.

23. "Development Process," *Common Core State Standards Initiative,* 2014, retrieved from http://www.corestandards.org/about-the-standards/development-process/.

24. U.S. Department of Education, National Center for Education Statistics, "The Condition of Education 2014 (NCES 2014-083), Status Dropout Rates," retrieved from http://nces.ed.gov/fastfacts/display.asp?id=16.

25. Ibid.

26. National Indian Education Association. (2014). Statistics on NAtive Students. http://www.niea.org/Research/statistics.aspx#studentDemographics.

27. "High School Dropout Statistics," *Statistic Brain,* January 1, 2014, retrieved from http://www.statisticbrain.com/high-school-dropout-statistics/.

28. L. Layton, "GAO: 40 States Have Suspected Cheating on K–12 Tests," *The Washington Post,* May 17, 2013, retrieved from http://www.washingtonpost.com/local/education/gao-40-states-have-suspected-cheating-on-k-12-tests/2013/05/17/a366542c-bf1d-11e2-97d4-a479289a31f9_story.html.

29. L. Copeland, "School Cheating Scandal Shakes Up Atlanta," *USA Today,* April 14, 2014, retrieved from http://www.usatoday.com/story/news/nation/2013/04/13/atlanta-school-cheatring-race/2079327/.

30. M. Winerip, "Ex-Schools Chief in Atlanta Is Indicted in Testing Scandal," *New York Times,* March 29, 2013, retrieved from http://www.nytimes.com/2013/03/30/us/former-school-chief-in-atlanta-indicted-in-cheating-scandal.html?pagewanted=all&_r=0.

31. Ibid.

32. Kappes, 2012.

33. C. Sanchez, "El Paso Schools Cheating Scandal: Who's Accountable?" *National Public Radio,* April 10, 2013, retrieved from http://www.npr.org/2013/04/10/176784631/el-paso-schools-cheating-scandal-probes-officials-accountability.

34. "Economic Impacts of Dropouts," *National Dropout Prevention Center/Network,* 2013, retrieved from http://www.dropoutprevention.org/statistics/quick-facts/economic-impacts-dropouts.

35. C. W. Harlow, *Education and Correctional Populations* (Washington, D.C.: U.S. Department of Justice, 2003).

36. J. T. Dahlburg, "Web of Scandal Ensnares Florida Prison System," *Los Angeles Times,* April 2, 2006, retrieved from http://articles.latimes.com/2006/apr/02/nation/na-prisons2.

37. Ibid.

38. "Kitchen Supervisor Gets Prison Time for Sexually Abusing Two Prisoners," *Prison Legal News,* April 15, 2014), retrieved from https://www.prisonlegalnews.org/news/2014/apr/15/kitchen-supervisor-gets-prison-time-for-sexually-abusing-two-prisoners/.

39. Ibid.

40. M. Clarke and A. Friedman, "State-by-State Prisoner Rape and Sexual Abuse Round-Up," *Prison Legal News,* April 15, 2012, retrieved from https://www.prisonlegalnews.org/news/2012/apr/15/state-by-state-prisoner-rape-and-sexual-abuse-round-up/

41. M. Gray, "Racketeering, Smuggling, Sex with Guards: 25 Indicted In Massive Baltimore Prison Scandal," *Time,* April 24, 2013, retrieved from http://nation.time.com/2013/04/24/sex-with-guards-in-baltimore-prison-scandal/.

42. A. Marimow and J. Wagner, "13 Corrections Officers Indicted in Md., Accused of Aiding Gang's Drug Scheme," *Washington Post,* April 23, 2013, retrieved from http://www.washingtonpost.com/local/thirteen-correctional-officers-indicted-in-maryland/2013/04/23/6d2cbc14-ac23-11e2-a8b9-2a63d75b5459_story.html.

43. San Antonio Independent School District v. Rodriguez, 337 F. US Supp 280, December 23, 1971.

44. Name changed to protect privacy.

EIGHT

Charter Schools versus Private Prisons

In recent years, solutions to the public school and prison problems have appeared in the form of charter schools and for-profit prisons. Many opponents of the public schools and the current prison systems believe that by allowing these alternative options, a competitive market will force the struggling systems to change to compete with newer ideas. While in theory, this idea sounds great, problems have arisen in the two institutions that have been formed as competitors for public schools and prisons. This chapter discusses charter schools and their influence on the public education system, and the influence of charter schools' partner, for-profit prisons, on public prisons.

The idea of charter schools can be traced back to Dr. Ray Budde, a professor at the University of Massachusetts at Amherst. In 1988, Dr. Budde wrote a report, *Education by Charter*, in which he outlined a plan for schools to move away from being administratively led to being led by teachers.[1] It was not until President George H. W. Bush's education plan, *America 2000*, which offered parents publicly funded vouchers to enroll their students in private schools, that charters became a viable option.

In 1991, Minnesota was the first state to pass laws allowing charter schools. Between 2010 and 2011, forty-one states and the District of Columbia all passed legislation allowing charter schools. Today, forty-two states and the District of Columbia allow charter schools. The eight states without charter school legislation are Alabama, Kentucky, Montana, Nebraska, North Dakota, South Dakota, Vermont, and West Virginia.[2] A charter school is defined by the National Center for Education Statistics as a "publicly funded school that is typically governed by a group or organization under a legislative contract or charter with the state or jurisdiction."[3] Charter schools are exempt from certain state and local regulations; however, in their charter with the local governing body, charter schools set out specific accountability standards in exchange for funding and autonomy.[4] Charter documents and the school's progress toward meeting the goals outlined in the charter are normally reviewed every three to five years; if the charter school is not meeting its goals, the governing body can revoke the charter and close the school.[5] The governing body of a charter school can also close the school if the curriculum or management guidelines are not being followed accurately.[6]

People confuse charter schools with private schools, which is a troubling mistake. Charter schools are publicly funded and do not charge tuition to their students, while private schools rely on tuition money and funding from nonpublic entities like churches. A third type of school is the magnet school. Magnet schools are also public schools, but they are highly selective and specialized. Schools considered magnet schools normally specialize in a specific area of content, such as mathematics, science, or the arts. Students who attend magnet schools have completed a rigorous testing and application process and possibly even an audition. While magnet and private schools are popular, charter schools have exploded in popularity, especially since they are free and relatively easy to enter.

As mentioned previously, states set the laws governing charter schools. This means that each state allows different groups to create charter schools. In most states, universities and nonprofit groups are allowed to form charter schools. Some states even allow for-profit groups to start charter schools. To create a charter school, a group must apply to the appropriate authorizing authorities; these authorities vary from state to state. Once the charter group is approved, the charter school group must create school plans and goals that meet the criteria set forth by the governing body. If the plan is approved, then typically the charter is granted for three to five years with periodic performance reviews built into the charter. If a charter school is struggling and up for renewal, then the charter can be granted for a year and reviewed for signs of progress.

Funding for charter schools has created much animosity among supporters of public schools and charter schools. Although state laws determine the funding for charter schools, most charter schools are funded with taxpayer dollars. Charter schools receive a portion of the money that goes to public schools. This division angers supporters of both institutions. Public school supporters believe that this loss of revenue erodes the public school system by furthering economic troubles for public schools. Supporters of charter schools complain that the percentage they receive per student is too low. This complaint was recently examined by a study done at the University of Arkansas,[7] which showed differences in monies received by charter schools as small as $365 a year in New Mexico and as large as $12,736 in Washington D.C.[8] Although this study has come under much criticism, the reality is still unknown.[9]

The study also found that between 2007 and 2011, charter schools lost 10.8 percent of their funding versus public schools, which lost 4.8 percent.[10] This loss disparity has to do with the federal government and other funding resources increasing for public schools.[11] In 2011 alone, charter schools received $3,000 less per student than public schools, which translated into a $1.5 million dollar deficit for an average-sized charter school per year.[12] While these statistics for funding may seem dismal for charter schools, many schools, both charter and public, actively seek contributions from companies to supplement their deficiencies.

The mission of charter schools is not vastly different from the mission of public schools. However, the way charter schools go about providing their education may differ greatly from public schools. When creating their charters with the charter granting authorities in the state, the group beginning the charter will lay out specific curriculum goals that the school will accomplish. The charter will specify how the school will measure success. Students who are enrolled in charter schools must complete state educational testing and are held to standards set by the local and state boards of education.

Charter schools are able to approach how they educate children differently than public schools. For example, some charter schools focus on attracting low-performing students who struggle in public schools. Other charter schools focus on students with disabilities or students who are interested in the arts, mathematics and science, writing, the military, or other interests. Whatever the charter focuses on, the students are still required to receive a basic[13] education. To accomplish these goals, charters can assign students individual projects, group work, additional classes, and other options that are not available in public schools. For example, Western New York Maritime Charter School (WNYMCS) describes itself as "An academic and naval science program designed to instill in cadets the highest sense of morality and ethics with emphasis on integrity, discipline, honor, and service to others."[14]

The WNYMCS completes its mission by using a naval code of conduct to perform day-to-day routines at the school. Every student at the WNYMCS is also a member of the Navy Junior Reserve Officer Training Corps (NJROTC) and participates in drills, color guards, and other activities sanctioned by the NJROTC. Students are offered classes in sailing as well as boat building, and are held to the naval code of conduct standards. Many of the administrators of the WNYMCS are former members of the Navy and Marines. While some charter schools like WNYMCS are similar to traditional public schools, by conducting classes and having a physical location, new types of charter schools, like cyber charter schools have appeared.

Enrollment in a charter school is not difficult; however, most states require that a student enroll in only one school at a time. Normally, when parents choose to enroll their child in a charter school, they notify the school that they are withdrawing their student and moving them to a charter school. However, until the public school receives official notification from the charter school that the new student has been enrolled, the student is still a member of the public school. Once the public school receives the notice of enrollment from the charter school, then the student is released from the public school. Unlike public schools, who must accept all students who live within the district, charter schools are able to accept and deny students based on the school's criteria, student's prior behavior, and academic records.

This ability to be selective has caused supporters of public schools to criticize charter schools, bemoaning the fact that public schools must accept all students, regardless of their issues, which they believe puts public schools at a disadvantage on state and national tests. Research has been conducted on charter schools since the first charter school opened in Minnesota and most of the research is inconclusive. Some research has shown that charter schools are more successful and graduate more students than public schools, while other research shows that this statement is false. Other studies have examined test scores, future career paths, and educational attainment of charter school students versus public school students and the answers have remained murky and indecisive. Some of this lack of clarity stems from the different rules governing charter schools, the unique missions of each school, and the transiency of students between charter schools and public schools.

During the 2011–2012 school year there were almost six thousand charter schools, up from the almost two thousand in the 1999–2000 school year.[15] During this same time period, enrollment increased from 0.3 million to 2.1 million students.[16] Between the 2010–2011 and 2011–2012 school year alone, charter school attendance increased by 0.3 million.[17] Supporters of charter schools argue that charter schools give students more educational opportunities, aggressively pursue student growth, provide smaller classrooms, and allow greater classroom innovation and more student involvement.[18] The National Alliance for Public Charter Schools claims that charter schools are some of the top performing schools in the country; are closing the achievement gap; and are getting more students accepted into colleges and universities by adjusting the curriculum to fit all students, creating a healthy school culture, and developing new state-of-the-art learning models.[19]

Those who oppose charter schools claim that the autonomy granted to charter schools in their charter agreement creates a system of schooling that has very little oversight and regulation. According to the Education Commission of the States, opponents of charter schools have four main issues.[20] First, since charter schools are run like businesses, they are subject to economic market forces to keep the school up and running. When market forces change, the charter can be forced to close without notice, disrupting the educational experiences of the students within that charter. A second problem that opponents have with charter schools is the propensity to segregate students. Research is currently emerging on this topic that shows that charter schools have a tendency to segregate based on race, socioeconomic status, or language proficiency.

A third concern that opponents of charter schools have is that student progress is hard to measure and enforce. Charter schools are faced with the dilemma of meeting state demands for accountability and the public's demand for educational opportunities not offered in the public schools; therefore, creating a successful system that measures student achievement is difficult. The fourth complaint has centered on the emergence of educational management organizations (EMOs), which remove decision-making ability from the local community. These EMOs run charter schools as a business, defeating the original purpose of charter schools as a locally driven educational entity.

Other complaints about charter schools have emerged, but many of these are based on state charter laws. Some of these complaints include teachers in charter schools not being certified, students who transfer from a charter school to a public school not being on educational grade level, students who transfer tending to have difficulty adjusting to the social and emotional aspects of public school, low standards for students, difficulty serving students with disabilities, and concerns that charter schools are more interested in making a profit than educating students. However, what needs to be understood about charter schools is that all charter schools are unique. Some charter schools are doing an amazing job providing a successful educational experience to their students, while others are struggling to provide the basics. It is unfair to say that all charter schools are bad or exceptional; each charter school must be judged with an eye on the goals laid out in its charter, the educational attainment of its students, and the ability of its students to lead a successful life after graduation.

What we must remember about charter schools is that they were born out of a desire to improve and offer competition to public schools. This competition is supposed to improve public schools. Yes, some parents will still want to enroll their child in a charter school anyway, whether it is for the special programs offered, like those at WNYMCS, or other specialty issues, but if public schools can offer an education that is beyond compare, few parents will be willing to leave public schools. Instead of spending time and energy attacking charter schools, public schools should spend their time and energy creating the best public schools possible.

Turning the focus from critiquing competitors to creating the best possible public system is also relevant for the prison system. A theory that has emerged from research for the reliance on prisons as a form of punishment postulates that the dominant class uses prison as a form of social, political, and economic control over those that the dominant class

deems dangerous; this includes the poor, unemployed, homeless, mentally ill, racial others, and political dissidents.[21] However, many will argue
that this statement is false and that prisons are used to punish those who
commit crimes, regardless of socioeconomic status, employment, race, or
political views. Which version to believe is your choice; the point of the
problem is where all these inmates are housed.

President Ronald Reagan in 1981 declared that drug abuse was public
enemy number one and began the War on Drugs. Prior to President
Reagan's speech, the 1960s had shown a rising trend in drug use by
White, middle class youth as a way to protest and create social unrest.[22]
This rise in drug use by the middle class lessened the social stigmatiza-
tion of drugs. When Nixon ran for President in 1968, he ran on a campaign that called for law and order, particularly in the area of drug use.
This launching of the drug war coincided with the crack cocaine epidemic in inner-city communities. In the 1950s and 1960s, manufacturing jobs
were plentiful in city centers and urban areas; young men with a basic
education could find work in the factories.

However, with the economic downturn in the 1970s and manufacturing companies moving their jobs to the suburbs, inner-city inhabitants
were left without jobs and incomes. This decline in legitimate employment led to opportunities for employment in various illegal enterprises,
specifically in the crack cocaine trade. Crack cocaine is a version of pow-
dered cocaine that can be vaporized and inhaled for an immediate high;
since it is inhaled, less of the drug can be used, making it possible to sell
smaller doses for more affordable prices.[23] Crack cocaine sped through
urban communities leaving destruction, devastation, and suffering in its
wake.

President Nixon chose to address the problem of crack not by offering
treatment or rehabilitation, but by prosecuting and sentencing drug offenders to prison time. Other countries, like Portugal, chose to decrimi-
nalize drugs (this does not mean drugs are legal in Portugal; it just means
possession of certain drugs, under a certain amount, does not result in
criminal charges or prison time).[24] Instead, in Portugal, first time offenders and those carrying under the legal amount are offered drug counseling and rehabilitation services; those carrying over the legal amount are
charged criminally, sentenced to prison time, and rehabilitation.[25] By
choosing to prosecute and incarcerate those caught with drugs, the United States created a multi-billion dollar police and prison system. In September 1986, President Reagan signed the first Anti-Drug Abuse Act into
law. This Act set mandatory minimum sentences for the distribution of
drugs, with a special emphasis on crack cocaine. This special emphasis on
crack cocaine dealers targeted African-American urban men.

In 1988, President Reagan once again revisited the Anti-Drug Abuse
Act, creating civil penalties for drug offenders. These civil penalties included eviction from public housing for allowing drug activity to occur

in or near a residence in public housing and exclusion from federal benefits, including student loans.[26] This new Act also included the death penalty for serious drug offenses and a five-year minimum prison sentence
for possession of cocaine base; this new five-year minimum would apply
to first-time offenders.[27] President George H. W. Bush continued this
tough-on-crime trend; however, it was not until President William Clinton took office that the effects of the War on Drugs and a tough-on-crime
mentality were seen.

During William (Bill) Clinton's tenure as Governor of Arkansas, he
had been accused by opposing candidates as being soft on crime. To
combat that image and secure the votes needed for the presidency, right
before the New Hampshire primary (a crucial primary for presidential
votes) Governor Clinton flew home to oversee the execution of Ricky Ray
Rector. Mr. Rector was convicted in 1982 for two murders, one a police
officer, in Conway, Arkansas.[28] After shooting the police officer, Mr. Rector attempted to commit suicide, shooting himself in the head. However,
emergency room staff were able to save Mr. Rector's life. At the trial,
conflicting experts testified to the mental state of Mr. Rector; the judge's
final verdict was that Mr. Rector was competent to stand trial. After being
tried and convicted, Mr. Rector was sentenced to death. In 1992, Govern-
or Clinton flew back to Arkansas to be present at Mr. Rector's execution.
It is said that the night before the execution when Mr. Rector was served
his last meal, he put his dessert aside, claiming he was saving it for the
next morning.[29] Mr. Rector's execution was successfully carried out on
January 24, 1992, at 10:09 pm central time, the beginning of President
Clinton's tough stance on crime.

In 1994, President Clinton signed a 30 billion dollar crime bill that
created dozens of new capital crimes, created the "three strikes and
you're out law," and authorized more than 16 billion dollars for the construction and expansion of new prisons and the growth of police forces.[30]
The "three strikes and you're out law" meant that anyone who had been
convicted of two or more prior violent crimes or serious felonies and was
convicted of another felony (a third), was not eligible for sentences other
than life in prison. The "three strikes and you're out" law was applied to
many drug offenses, since drug charges were considered felonies. Consider the case of Leandro Andrade, a California father of three who is
now in prison for two consecutive life sentences for shoplifting nine children's videos on two separate occasions in 1995.[31] In California alone, the
Shouse Law Group estimates that one in four inmates were sentenced to
significant prison time because of the "three strikes and you're out"
law.[32]

President Clinton affixed further penalties to those convicted of drug
offenses. Those convicted of drug-related offenses received a lifetime ban
on food stamps and President Clinton made it easier for public housing
to evict and exclude those convicted of drug offenses.[33] During Clinton's

administration, he slashed the budget for public housing and increased the budget for building prisons. [34]

In 1980, 19,023 people were incarcerated in federal prisons and 4,749 of those people, approximately 25 percent, were incarcerated for drug offenses. [35] Twenty-nine years later, in 2009, 187,886 people were incarcerated in federal prisons and 95,205 were incarcerated for drug offenses, an increase of approximately 51 percent. [36] In federal prisons, drug offenders are over half of the prison population and constitute the most significant source of growth in the federal prison system; over half of those incarcerated are incarcerated for drug offenses and the majority are minorities. [37] Between 1980 and 2013, the Federal Bureau of Prison's (BOP) numbers increased from approximately 25,000 to 219,000, an increase of approximately 6,000 inmates per year. [38] With this drastic increase in inmates came a large increase in funding; BOP appropriations increased from $3.668 billion to $6.445 billion; and the average cost to house an inmate rose from $21,603 to $29,291. [39]

The rising number of inmates and cost of incarceration has severely taxed the federal and state prison system. Overall, federal prisons are operating at 36 percent over capacity with some high- and medium-security facilities operating at 52 percent and 45 percent over capacity. [40] These over-capacity operations can lead to dangerous situations for correctional officers since they are often outnumbered 9.9 to 1. [41] It is estimated that there are 159 prison modernization and repair projects that need to take place, at an estimated cost of $342 million. [42] These projects would do little to ease the overcrowding currently taking place in federal prisons; to alleviate federal overcrowding, more prisons need to be built, other rehabilitative measures need to be taken, or more inmates need to be placed in private prisons. Currently 173,606 inmates are incarcerated in BOP-operated facilities; another 29,125 inmates are incarcerated in privately operated facilities. [43]

One of the largest private corrections firms in the United States is the Corrections Corporation of America (CCA). CCA began in 1983 when T. Don Hutto, a former correctional officer and counselor who became a prison warden, joined forces with Tom Beasley and Dr. Robert Crants, both former West Point graduates and lawyers. [44] Their idea was to create a private prison that ran on strict accountability and rigorous guidelines, contained strong oversight, and met high standards to work in conjunction with government partners to ease the strain on public prisons. Since CCA operated independently from the government, the corporation could design, finance, operate, and manage prisons based on the specific needs of their government contracts. CCA was awarded its first contract with the U.S. Department of Justice building the Houston Processing Center for Immigration and Naturalization Services. [45]

CCA has existed for more than thirty years and now operates sixty facilities in twenty-one states plus the District of Columbia, employs

14,000 people,[46] and in 2010 reported revenues exceeding $2.9 billion.[47] With a growing national debt and an expanding prison population, commentators in the 1990s and early 2000s viewed private prisons as an answer to the overcrowded and failing public prisons system. Three private prison companies emerged as the major players in the private prison industry, the largest being CCA, followed by the GEO Group (formerly Wackenhut Securities), and finally Community Education Centers, the third largest.

Private prison supporters subscribe to the same arguments as charter school supporters: With more options come more competition, and competition means cost savings and better opportunities. The premise of private prisons has revolved around the idea that they will be able to reduce the cost of housing inmates, saving states and the federal government money. Issues of overcrowding and violence would be solved as private prisons alleviate the burden on the public system. Another benefit claimed by the private prison industry is that these new private prisons could be built in rural communities to boost their economies. With growing national and state debts and increasing budgets for corrections, the promises made by private prison corporations seemed like a solution to a nationwide problem. However, problems soon arose as private prison corporations struggled to fulfill their promises.

Five main issues arose with private prisons. The first issue that arose was the actual promise of cost savings, which was the premier concept of private prisons. Research has shown that while private prisons may save some in costs, this cost cutting comes with a high price for staff and inmates.[48] It is worth noting here that the information and research available on public and private prisons is not totally encompassing or equal. While public prisons are required to make almost all of their information available to the public, private prisons may pick and choose what information is made available.

Since labor costs are one of the main expenditures of prisons, private prisons have chosen this area as a focus for cost cutting. Private prisons pay less, provide fewer benefits, hire nonunion workers, require, and give less training to their correctional officers than public prisons.[49] Correctional officers at private prisons are not given qualified immunity, which means that unlike their public counterparts, private prison correctional officers can be named as defendants in lawsuits.[50] To reduce costs, private prisons have fewer administrative layers, which can reduce bureaucracy but also puts the organization at risk for lack of oversight. By cutting the cost of staff labor in private prisons, many private prisons have had increased issues with violence.

A second problem with the promises made by private prisons deals with cost savings. Part of the lure of private prisons was that options would abound and competition would help drive down costs as private prisons competed for state and federal bids. However, the reality is far different. In the United States, two major corporations have evolved as the clear winners in the private prison market. CCA is the leading company pulling in over $2.9 billion dollars in 2010, followed closely by The GEO Group. A few, much smaller companies also exist, but are rarely considered for federal contracts or even large state contracts. Therefore, a system that was created because it offered choices and competition has been taken over by two large companies, limiting the choices and competition.

A third issue with private prisons has been the way that the contracts work between the federal or state government and the private prison corporation. While exact details on the specifics of contracts between private prisons and the contracting body are not made public, what is known about these contracts is disturbing. Federal contracts offer terms that are much more favorable to private prisons than those offered by state governments. Since the contracts depend on the percentage of inmates housed in private prisons, private prisons often receive bonuses once the percentage is reached.

Rahr found that "once a facility population exceeds 50 percent of the contract capacity, the BOP pays the private operator a fixed monthly operating price for the remainder of the contract. The private operator therefore earns the increment regardless of whether the actual future inmate population is 51 percent or 89 percent of contract capacity."[51] This is also true when the private prison reaches 90 percent of its contracted number.[52] Public prisons, however, are funded based on the actual number of inmates within the prison, not the percentage. This differential can encourage private prisons to meet the minimum threshold so that they are given their bonus, while allowing them to avoid taking on more inmates. This tactic has done little to relieve the overcrowding of state and federal prisons, as private prisons have promised.

The fourth issue that has arisen with private prisons has been oversight and accountability. The majority of private prison contracts require that the prison show an annual savings of 5 to 10 percent.[53] While one would think that this would be a relatively simple task, that is far from the truth. While private prisons can show reductions in staff costs and various other expenses, private prisons incur many other hidden fees. Due to the savings found in cutting staff costs, private prisons are subjected to more outside monitoring, inspections, and trainings than public prisons.[54] While public prisons are required to collect this aggregate data and publish it, private prisons are not required to either collect or display the data; this data is also not required when the contractor selects a private prison.

An issue related to oversight and accountability is the type of inmates who are often contracted for and accepted by private prisons. The majority of private prisons house inmates that are minimum to medium security. Almost 90 percent of private prison populations are made up of inmates that are minimum- or medium-security levels, compared with almost 70 percent of the public sector.[55] Inmates with a lower security rating, like a minimum or medium, are less expensive to incarcerate than those who are categorized as high-risk. Since private prisons can contract out for the types of inmates they will house, most choose those whose security risks are lower because they are cheaper to incarcerate and need less supervision and security, thereby cutting prison costs.

The last issue that has arisen from promises made by the private prison industry is their promise that their companies will promote job creation and economic stimulation in small, impoverished, rural areas. With the decline of manufacturing and agriculture, many rural communities have struggled financially. Private prison corporations have targeted these struggling communities, promising that with the construction of a prison, jobs will be available and an economic upswing will commence. The reality, however, is not so rosy. Since private prisons use cuts to employee salaries and benefits as a way to lower costs, those who choose to work for the private prison make less than their public counterparts. The stability of private prisons jobs is also an issue; the turnover rate for private prison jobs (40.9 percent) is almost three times that of public prisons (15.4 percent).[56]

Private prisons further compound economic problems for rural communities. When a community builds a prison and invites a for-profit company to staff the facility, often large corporate stores like Walmart and Target move into town, driving out local businesses. Another financial burden is added when the influx of new people drawn by the promise of work move to the community. Rent prices increase, leaving many poor and elderly people in dire financial and housing situations.[57] Since inmates are required to work and their labor is incredibly cheap, many times the prison can offer goods for much lower prices than local businesses, causing many businesses to fold.

Rural communities are also responsible for what happens when there is a problem inside or with the prison. The farming town of Littlefield in West Texas borrowed $10 million dollars to build their prison; they then rented the building out to The GEO Group.[58] For two years, the prison brought in revenue by housing inmates from Idaho and Wyoming, but Idaho suddenly withdrew their contract. Soon, the GEO Group notified Littlefield that they too would be pulling out of the prison. The Littlefield prison has sat empty ever since. The town still has to pay a 65,000 dollar note each month on the prison; that is 10 additional dollars per person for each person in the town.[59]

A perfect example of these five issues happened in Youngstown, Ohio, a former steel town that had fallen on economic hard times when the steel mills left. Good jobs are hard to find here, and the economy has stagnated. The city of Youngstown cheaply sold land to the CCA. The prison opened in 1997 and had a contract with the Department of Corrections in Washington, D.C., to acquire 1,500 minimum-security inmates.[60] In its first fourteen months of operation, two inmates were stabbed to death and multiple inmates were injured in other stabbing incidents.

An investigation revealed that due to lax screening procedures, over one hundred dangerous inmates requiring a high security level were sent to the Northeast Ohio Correctional Center (NEOCC). One of the reasons that has emerged for the lax screening of inmates was the speed in which inmates were transferred. In a little over two weeks more than nine hundred inmates had been transferred.[61] On one day alone, 156 inmates had been transferred to NEOCC from other prisons.[62] The second reason found that correctional officers were poorly trained and completely overwhelmed. Inmates at NEOCC filed a lawsuit against CCA and won.

In July 1998, six inmates escaped from NEOCC and were eventually recaptured. In 2013, CCA was forced by the BOP to rebid for the NEOCC contract and told city officials that they would like to consolidate to one prison in a seven-state radius. Youngstown city officials are desperate to keep the prison and have promoted the economic importance of the prison. Officials cite the 440 jobs that would be lost, as well as $1.9 million dollars in property taxes (of which officials cite $1.3 million going toward Youngstown City schools), $20 million in payroll and benefits (approximately $50,000 per employee), and the $1.2 million spent on goods and services ($600,000 spent on local businesses).[63] The decision is expected anytime, but will occur before February 2015. Recently, the American Civil Liberties Union has been protesting renewing NEOCC's contract since the prison is used to house undocumented immigrants.[64]

While many people believe that charter schools and private prisons offer competition and opportunities that will force the public system to change and improve, the reality has not been as bright. These alternative opportunities have created unique problems of their own. Public schools and prisons have focused more on complaining and bemoaning than on evaluating and fixing their own institutions. However, my worries focus on what we view as acceptable alternates. Are exemptions, lack of oversight, cost-saving measures, and less accountability the direction we hope to move in? If we are unhappy with the current system, why are we not making meaningful changes? What will it take to make meaningful change? Can the system even change? While these are all pertinent questions, the answers are elusive. Change is accomplished slowly and with persistence. Are we willing?

NOTES

1. *Federal Education Policy and the States, 1945–2009* (New York: New York State Education Department, 2006).

2. The Center for Education Reform, retrieved from www.edreform.com.

3. National Center for Education Statistics, 2014, retrieved from http://nces.ed.gov/

4. Ibid.

5. Ibid.

6. Ibid.

7. M. Batdorff, L. Maloney, J. May, S. Speakman, P. Wolf, A. Cheng, *The Productivity of Public Charter Schools* (Fayetteville, AR: School Choice Demonstration Project, University of Arkansas, 2014).

8. Ibid.

9. . W. J. Mathis and B. Baker, "Erroneousness Expands," National Education Policy Center, May 20, 2014, retrieved from http://nepc.colorado.edu/newsletter/2014/05/review-charter-funding-inequity.

10. Batdorff et al., *The Productivity of Public Charter Schools.*

11. Ibid.

12. Ibid.

13. Subjects like reading, writing, mathematics, literature, science, and social studies.

14. Western New York Maritime Charter School, retrieved from http://www.wnymcs9-12.com/site/default.aspx?PageID=1.

15. *The Condition of Education,* National Center for Education Statistics, April 2014, retrieved from http://nces.ed.gov/pubsearch/pubsinfo.asp?pubid=2014083.

16. Ibid.

17. Ibid.

18. Editorial Projects in Education Research Center, "Issues A–Z: Charter Schools," *Education Week,* retrieved June, 12, 2014, from http://www.edweek.org/ew/issues/charter-schools/.

19. National Alliance for Public Charter School, *What Are Public Charter Schools?* 2014, retrieved from http://www.publiccharters.org/get-the-facts/public-charter-schools/.

20. "Choice of Schools—Charter Schools," *Education Commission of the States,* 2014, retrieved from http://www.ecs.org/html/issuesection.asp?issueid=20&s=pros+ percent26+cons.

21. T. Chang and D. E. Thompkins, "Corporation Go To Prison," *Journal of Labor Studies* 27, No. 1 (2002): 45–66; D. Jacobs and R. Helms, "Towards a Political Sociology of Punishment: Politics and Changes in the Incarcerated Population," *Social Science Research,* 30, Summer (2002): 171–194; C. Parenti, *Lockdown America: Police and Prisons in the Age of Crisis* (New York: Verso, 1999).

22. "Thirty Years of America's Drug War: A Chronology," *Frontline,* retrieved from http://www.pbs.org/wgbh/pages/frontline/shows/drugs/cron/.

23. M. Alexander, *The New Jim Crow: Mass Incarceration in the Age of Blindness* (New York: The New Press, 2010).

24. W. Hollerson, "'This Is Working': Portugal, 12 Years after Decriminalizing Drugs," *Spiegel Online International,* March 27, 2013, retrieved from http://www.spiegel.de/international/europe/evaluating-drug-decriminalization-in-portugal-12-years-later-a-891060.html.

25. Ibid.

26. Alexander, *The New Jim Crow.*

27. Ibid.

28. P. Applebome, "The 1992 Campaign: Death Penalty; Arkansas Execution Raises Questions on Governor's Politics," *New York Times,* January 25, 1992, retrieved from http://www.nytimes.com/1992/01/25/us/1992-campaign-death-penalty-arkansas-execution-raises-questions-governor-s.html.

29. Alexander, *The New Jim Crow.*

30. Ibid.

31. "California Three Strikes Law and Proposition 36 Reform," Shouse Law Group, retrieved from http://www.shouselaw.com/three-strikes.html.

32. Ibid.

33. Alexander, *The New Jim Crow.*

34. Ibid.

35. "The Expanding Federal Prison Population," The Sentencing Project, March 2011, retrieved from http://www.sentencingproject.org/doc/publications/inc_FederalPrisonFactsheet_March2011.pdf.

36. Ibid.

37. Ibid.

38. N. James, "The Federal Prison Population Buildup: Overview, Policy Changes, Issues, and Options," *Congressional Research Service*, April 15, 2014, retrieved from http://www.fas.org/sgp/crs/misc/R42937.pdf.

39. Ibid.

40. Ibid.

41. Ibid.

42. Ibid.

43. "Statistics: Inmate Population Report," Federal Bureau of Prisons, June 19, 2014, retrieved from http://www.bop.gov/about/statistics/population_statistics.jsp.

44. "The CCA Story: Our Company History," Corrections Corporation of America, retrieved from http://cca.com/our-history.

45. Ibid.

46. Ibid.

47. C. Mason, "Too Good to Be True: Private Prisons in America," The Sentencing Project, 2012, retrieved from http://sentencingproject.org/doc/publications/inc_Too_Good_to_be_True.pdf.

48. R. Kish and A. Lipton, "Do Private Prisons Really Offer Savings Compared with Their Public Counterparts?" *Economic Affairs* 33, No. 1 (2013): 93–107.

49. Ibid.

50. Ibid.

51. S. Raher, "The Business of Punishing: Impediments to Accountability in the Private Corrections Industry," *Richmond Journal of Law and the Public Interest* 13, No. 2 (2010): 209–249.

52. Kish and Lipton, *Do Private Prisons Really Offer Savings Compared With Their Public Counterparts?*

53. Ibid.

54. D. C. McDonald, E. Fournier, M. Russell-Einhourn, and S. Crawford, *Private Prisons in the United States: An Assessment of Current Practice* (Cambridge, MA: Abt Associates, 1998), retrieved from http://www.abtassociates.com/reports/priv-report.pdf.

55. Mason, "To Good to Be True."

56. T. Huling, "Building a Prison Economy in Rural America," in eds. M. Mauer and M. Chensey-Lind, *From Invisible Punishment: The Collateral Consequences of Mass Imprisonment* (New York: The New Press, 2002).

57. Ibid.

58. J. Burnett, "Private Prison Promises Leave Texas Towns in Trouble," *National Public Radio*, March 28, 2011, retrieved from http://www.npr.org/2011/03/28/134855801/private-prison-promises-leave-texas-towns-in-trouble.

59. Ibid.

60. J. Clark, "Report to the Attorney General Inspection and Review of the Northeast Ohio Correctional Center," November 25, 2998, retrieved from http://www.justice.gov/ag/youngstown/youngstown.htm.

61. Ibid.

62. Ibid.

63. D. O'Brien, "CCA Prison Seeks Public Support in Contract Bid," *The Business Journal*, July 19, 2013, retrieved from http://businessjournaldaily.com/company-news/cca-prison-seeks-public-support-contract-bid-2013-7-19.

64. P. Milliken, "ACLU: BOP Should End NEOCC's Immigrant Inmate Contract," *Vindy.com*, June 11, 2014, retrieved from http://www.vindy.com/news/2014/jun/11/aclu-seeks-end-to-neocc-pact-to-house-im/.

NINE

School Discipline and Juvenile Justice

One and the Same?

The last major topic broached by this book is the comparison of school discipline and juvenile justice. These two complex systems are often linked together. When a youth in today's society violates a serious school rule, the youth may find himself or herself facing charges in the juvenile system. This chapter first explores school discipline policies with specific regard to suspension and expulsions, followed by an explanation of how the juvenile justice system works. Recently, school resource officers (SROs) have served as linking forces between schools and the court system. While research on the presence of SROs has been inconclusive at best, there is no denying that security measures are here to stay within our schools.

In 1994, as part of President Clinton's education plan, *Goals 2000: Educate America Act*, the Gun-Free School Act (GFSA) was passed. It was then reauthorized under the *Improving America's School Act*. The GFSA was another part of Clinton's get-tough-on-crime policy. According to a report published by the Office of Juvenile Justice and Delinquency Prevention, gun-related violence peaked in the 1980s and 1990s and has been steadily declining since.[1] While this may seem surprising, especially due to the media coverage of such events as the Columbine and Sandy Hook shootings, the school stabbings in Pennsylvania, and other school shootings, school gun violence and gun violence in general has been decreasing.[2] According to the National Association of School Psychologists, in the 2009–2010 school year the odds of a student being killed at school was one in 2.5 million.[3] In a study conducted by the U.S. Department of Justice, in the 1990s there were an average of twenty-nine school homicides per year; in the 2000s, this shrunk to an average of twenty per year.[4]

While this decline can be credited to numerous sources, the increase of gun violence (perceived or real) in the 1980s led to measures like the GFSA and Gun-Free School Zone Act (GFSZA) being passed. The first GFSZA was passed in 1990, prohibiting anyone from knowingly carrying or possessing a firearm in a school zone. In the Supreme Court Case, *United States v. Lopez,* the GFSZA was deemed unconstitutional by the Court since it violated the Commerce Clause in the United States Constitution. In 1996, the GFSZA was once again instituted, with a small change in wording, but still holding the same principles as the 1990 version. Attempts to challenge the provision have been made; however, the Supreme Court has held that the new version is constitutionally sound.

Clinton's version of the GFSA focused on the disciplining of students who brought weapons to school. GFSA mandated that a student who brought a weapon to school would face an immediate one-year expulsion. GFSA was required in all local education agencies (LEAs). The idea was to deter students from bringing weapons, but if the deterrent failed, punishment would be forthcoming. This policy quickly became known as a "zero-tolerance policy." Due to the mandates of the law, any weapon brought onto school property would immediately result in a student being expelled for an entire year. The media publicized horror stories about students being expelled for innocent mistakes like bringing a knife to slice an apple at lunch or a pocket knife that was forgotten. Even these simple mistakes or lapses in judgments resulted in students receiving a year's expulsion. Zero tolerance became the language of school discipline.

When No Child Left Behind (NCLB) was passed in 2001 under President George W. Bush, the GFSA was changed. According to NCLB, any state that received federal funding was required to have a law that mandated that LEAs have a policy that expelled students for a year if they brought or possessed a firearm at school. The term *school* was redefined and included school-sponsored events and activities, even if they were held off school grounds.[5] These changes loosened the zero-tolerance policy by allowing LEAs to provide some leeway on a case-by-case basis. NCLB and the new GFSA also authorized LEAs to provide an alternative education setting when a student was expelled. These changes universalized zero-tolerance policies but allowed some flexibility within the rules.

In the wake of highly publicized school shootings and stabbings, many schools have chosen to use the zero-tolerance policies as a starting point for their discipline policies. While each school district's discipline policies are unique, three strategies, detention, suspension, and expulsion, are used to handle most issues. Detention is normally used for small problems that arise like being tardy, misbehaving in class, class disruption, and other small failures in following the rules. Receiving detention means that the student is required to spend a set amount of time before or after school or on Saturdays sitting quietly in a classroom while a monitor observes and keeps the silence. Detention is the most used discipline procedure in schools and one of the least severe.

The second most frequently used discipline strategy in schools is suspension. Suspension is normally reserved for students who have violated a more serious rule or who have habitually violated the same rule and detention has not curbed the undesired behavior. When a suspension is issued, the student must be informed by the school of what violation occurred and the evidence the school has received of the violation, and the student has a right to speak and refute the claims. All of these can be done through verbal communication, but written notices need to be sent to the parent or guardian.

There are two types of suspension, in-school suspension (ISS) and out-of-school suspension (OSS). For ISS, students are isolated in a separate room with a monitor and forced to complete their assigned schoolwork in complete silence for the duration of the school day. ISS is used for students who need to be separated from the general school population for behavioral issues, but need not be completely removed from school. OSS is the removal of a student from school for a serious violation of the rules. Students who receive OSS are removed from the school property and all school-sponsored activities for the duration of the suspension.

There are certain rules that the school district must abide by when issuing a student OSS. These laws differ from state to state, but most are similar. Most states require that a student not be given OSS for more than ten days a year without a formal hearing. Depending on the rules of the state, these ten days can be either accumulated throughout the year or ten consecutive days. For example, if a student is suspended five different times for two days each time and is then facing a sixth suspension for two more days, a formal hearing must be called. Or, for example, if a student is facing a suspension for twelve consecutive days, a formal hearing must be called. Students with special needs are governed by different rules, discussed later.

Students can be suspended immediately after the incident or for a maximum of ten days. A student who is suspended for ten days can serve his or her ten-day suspension and reenter school. If a student is suspended for more than ten days, a meeting must occur; this meeting is called a *formal hearing* and involves the student's parents or guardians, a school administrator, or the school board. While every state and school district has different policies that govern suspensions, the universal consensus seems to be that after ten days, a formal hearing will happen. At the formal hearing, the best decision will be made that protects the safety of the school community while providing an education for the student involved. There does not seem to be a limit to how long a student can be suspended as long as a meeting has taken place between the parents or guardian of the students and a school representative.

Parents or guardians have the right to protest any suspension. During the formal hearing, the parent or guardian is allowed to bring an advocate. This advocate is usually more familiar with the policies and fights to make sure that the child's rights are protected. Advocates usually work for an agency like the American Civil Liberties Union or a parent who has taken on the cause, learned the rules, and will defend the student. All parents or guardians have the right to bring an advocate to meetings involving their child.

When a student with special needs is suspended, the first part of the process is exactly the same. The student must be notified verbally of his suspension and he or she has the right to present evidence to the contrary. However, when the suspension length reaches ten days, instead of having a formal hearing, the student has a manifestation determination meeting. This manifestation determination meeting includes the student, the student's parents or guardian, someone who can interpret the student's Individual Education Plan (IEP), and a school administrator. The purpose of this meeting is to determine if the negative behaviors involved are a result of the disability.

If it is determined that the negative behaviors are not caused by the disability, then the student can be subject to suspension. Special needs students, unlike regular students, must be provided educations services by their school district after their initial ten-day suspension is over. Should the manifestation determination meeting find that the negative behaviors are a result of the student's disability, then the IEP must be changed to accommodate the disability so that the student is not always subjected to discipline for that specific or related behavior. The manifestation determination meeting determines whether the student performs the negative behavior knowing that there will be consequences or scrutinizes whether the disability causes the student to not recognize the consequences of his or her actions. Other than the manifestation determination meeting, the process to suspend students with disabilities is the same as the process to suspend any other student. The manifestation determination meeting does not change or alter the suspension decision unless the negative behavior is a direct result of the student's disability or the school's failure to properly implement the IEP.

The third type of school discipline policy is school expulsion. Expelling a student from school is a serious matter because during the time the student is expelled from school, he or she cannot enroll in or attend any other school. This means that the student misses instructional time and, depending on the length of the expulsion, may lose credit for the entire year. Expulsion as a punishment is normally reserved for the most serious violations of school policy, like bringing a weapon to school, selling illegal drugs, or assault. If a student commits a felony, even outside of the school grounds, he or she can be subject to expulsion from school.

Since expulsion is such a serious discipline strategy, there are a few more policies regarding its use. Once again, the specifics of these policies depend on the state and the school district, but what follows is a general overview of the process. When a student has committed an act that violates one of the more serious school rules, depending on which policy the student has violated and the severity, the student may be removed from school immediately or can be suspended with intent to expel. Once again, a student who is expelled must have a formal hearing within ten days of being expelled. This formal hearing is the same as the formal hearing for a suspension; the student's parents or guardian are present as well as a school administrator or the school board.

Unlike suspensions, which are a less formal process, the expulsion process is governed by the Constitution. In the Supreme Court case *Goss v. Lopez* (1975), Dwight Lopez, a student at Central High School in Columbus, Ohio, was suspended along with seventy-five other students for a disturbance that broke out in their high school cafeteria, after which school officials claimed damage to the cafeteria had occurred.[6] Lopez claimed that he had not damaged any school property, yet he was suspended without a hearing or an explanation.

Simultaneously, Betty Chrome, who attended McGuffey Junior High School in Columbus, attended a protest held at another school; at this protest Betty was arrested, but released without charges and the next day learned she had been suspended for ten days without a hearing.[7] These two students joined other students who had been treated the same and together they filed a class action lawsuit against the Columbus Board of Education and the Columbus Public School System. The students alleged that their right to due process, included in the Fourteenth Amendment, had been violated when they were suspended without a hearing.

The trial court found in favor of the students and ordered the school district to remove the suspensions from the students' records. Unhappy with the decision, the schools appealed to the U.S. Supreme Court. In a five to four decision, the Supreme Court ruled in favor of the students, arguing that the due process clause was put in place to protect all citizens, even students. The Court also ruled that the right to attend school is a property right because of the value it provides. Suspending or expelling a student removes this property for a certain number of days and also harms a student's reputation, thereby affecting the student's liberty and freedom.[8] Therefore, because suspensions and expulsions violate a student's right to liberty, freedom, and property, due process is required for removal.

However, the Court did recognize that holding a due process hearing for every suspension was not feasible. Therefore, the Court made it mandatory for the school to notify the student of the allegations, explain the evidence against them, and give them an informal hearing. This informal hearing is normally a meeting between the principal and the student. In more serious cases, a formal hearing is needed. Expulsions, due to their serious nature, require a formal hearing.

A student facing expulsion and his parents or guardian must be notified in writing of the behaviors that are deemed expulsion worthy, the time, date, and place of the due process hearing, the right of the student to review his or her school records before the hearing, a description of the hearing procedures, and an explanation of what an expulsion entails.[9] Once a time, date, and place are agreed on, the due process hearing takes place. Due process meetings vary greatly depending on the school district and the state. Some schools treat the due process hearing similar to a court case, allowing the student facing expulsion to question opposing witnesses and provide their own witnesses. Others schools rely on a meeting between the student and the principal as the way to meet the due process mandate. Depending on the state, school board approval may be needed.

There are two options for expulsions. The first type of expulsion is a set day expulsion. This type of expulsion is normally used for weapons violations, assaults, or other severe violations. A set day expulsion means that a student is expelled for a set number of days up to one school year. If this type of expulsion happens, the student loses credit for the year that he is expelled and unless the student has an IEP, he will not receive educational services from the public school system. The second type of expulsion is an open-ended expulsion. This type of expulsion is often used for students who have violated the drug policies of the school. In this type of expulsion, the student is expelled for a certain number of days; however, a reentry plan is put into effect for the student. A reentry plan in these situations includes counseling, drug screening, substance abuse help, and other services deemed appropriate. Once the student has met the goals set out in the reentry plan, a meeting is convened and a reentry date can be established.

Students with disabilities can also be expelled; however, the rules for expulsion are different. The same rules apply to expulsion as suspensions; before the student has reached the tenth day of removal, a manifestation determination meeting must take place. At this meeting, it must be decided if the behavior in question is caused by the student's disability. If the behavior is determined to be caused by the disability, then the student's IEP must be reevaluated and changed to better reflect the needs of the child. If it is determined that the behavior is not part of the student's disability, the IEP does not need to be altered. Once again, this manifestation determination meeting does not affect the expulsion decision.

After the manifestation determination meeting, the student with special needs has the right to the same due process hearing as other students. At this due process hearing, if the parent or guardian of the student being expelled disagrees with the expulsion, then according to the Individuals with Disabilities Act (IDEA), the student can "stay put." *Staying put* means that while the school or law enforcement agency is investigating the incident, the student will stay in his current educational setting. If a special circumstance is involved, like bodily harm, weapons, or violence, the student can be placed in an interim alternative education setting (IAES). IAES includes home instruction or alternative school.

If the expulsion is for weapons or drugs and the student needs to be immediately removed, the student can be placed in IAES for forty-five days without parental consent. Once these forty-five days have elapsed, the student must be removed from IAES and placed back in the previous classroom setting. Students with an IEP are required to be given educational services during their expulsion. These services do not have to begin until after the ten days are over. Schools are required to provide a free and appropriate public education and the support services that are documented in the IEP when a student with special needs is expelled.

These support services often include "home instruction" as the method of delivery. If the manifestation determination meeting determines that the behavior is a direct result of the student's disability or the school's failure to implement properly the student's IEP, then the expulsion proceedings will halt, and an adjustment will be made to the student's IEP. If the behaviors are not linked to the student's disability or the school's failure to properly implement the IEP, then the student can be expelled, but educational services must be provided. The expulsion process varies from state to state and district to district for students without IEPs. However, for students with IEPs, the process is governed by IDEA.

In addition to these three forms of punishment, many schools have begun using SROs. These measures have gained in popularity due to school shootings and a need to create a feeling of safety and security for students, parents, and staff. An SRO is a law enforcement officer who is assigned to an elementary, middle, or high school to prevent juvenile delinquency and create positive bonds between youth and law enforcement officers.[10] In most school districts with SROs, the SRO is employed by the local law enforcement agency; however, in large city districts SROs can actually be employed by the district. According to the National Association of School Resource Officers, the SRO program is built around three main principles: an SRO is a teacher, counselor, and law enforcement officer.[11] Policing agencies and schools have always had an intertwined relationship; however, it has only been within the last two decades that SROs have become prevalent.

The first documented instance of an SRO was in Flint, Michigan in the 1950s, but instances of police involvement in schools can be traced as far back as 1939 in Indianapolis, Indiana.[12] Many researchers believe SROs have gained in popularity due to the widely publicized school shootings that have occurred since the 1990s. Identifying an accurate number of the SROs currently assigned to schools is difficult, but it is estimated that there are over twenty thousand SROs in schools today.[13] While some community members see the addition of SROs to schools in a positive light, many worry about the effect of bringing armed police officers into schools.

Those who support placing SROs in schools believe that SROs discourage students from bringing weapons and drugs into schools, as well as provide an extra layer of safety and security. Supporters stress that SROs play three important roles in the schools that they police. The first role is the role of the safety officer, which includes issuing citations and making arrests; controlling crime, gang, and drug activity; helping as a hall monitor and truancy enforcer; and serving as the liaison between the school and the police department.[14] The second role that supporters believe the SRO plays is that of the community resource contact. In this role SROs help to coordinate crime prevention programs, as well as coordinate efforts and initiatives that will make the school and community safer.[15] The third role played by an SRO is that of educator. In this role SROs educate students about alcohol and drug safety, conflict resolution, and other issues that may arise concerning the safety of students.[16]

Opponents of SROs in schools have worried about the effect of armed police officers in schools. Many opponents worry that armed police officers send the wrong message to students, treating the students like prison inmates or those confined to psychiatric hospitals. At issue, too, is the financial burden assumed by the school district when an SRO is hired. Since SRO salaries are paid by the school district, the cost of employing an SRO can add an increased financial burden to the school. The largest issue that many opponents cite as problematic is the SRO's involvement in creating and enforcing school discipline policies. Whereas school discipline was once handled by teachers and school administrators, that power has been taken away and given to the SRO and law enforcement agencies. This has taken away all the discretionary power that teachers and school administrators once held; now students are subjected to laws that offer little leniency.

Since the placement of SROs in schools is relatively new, the research on the effects of SROs in schools has shown mixed results. Several studies have shown that SROs have a positive influence in school, decreasing issues with drugs and gangs, while other studies have shown that SROs funnel more students into the juvenile justice system. Further research is being conducted on the effects of SROs in schools, however, this research will take time since it is difficult to pinpoint and attribute results to one particular person within a complex system. The effectiveness or ineffectiveness of SROs is not up for debate here; however, SROs and their link to police agencies sometimes result in students being turned over to the juvenile justice system for breaking the school policies that would have previously been handled within the school.

When juveniles enters the juvenile justice system, they go through an intake process. During this intake process the prosecution and defense gather information about the incident in question, the seriousness of the offense, and previous criminal or court history. If the juvenile has a previous criminal record, the court examines the success or failure of the rehabilitation selected for the previous offense. With this information compiled and examined, the court or prosecutor then chooses one of three options for how the case will be handled.

The first way to handle a case is to dismiss it. A dismissal is normally reserved for offenses that are less serious or have been handled improperly, or when the juvenile seeks help on his or her own terms. Secondly, prosecutors or courts can also recommend that the case be handled informally. When a case is handled informally, the juvenile agrees to specific conditions for a precise amount of time. Once the terms are agreed, a formal agreement between the prosecutor, courts, and the juvenile is signed, and the juvenile is assigned a probation officer who will monitor and ensure that the juvenile is fulfilling the terms of the agreement. Examples of informal handling include curfews, restitution, counseling, schooling, or community service.

In the third option, juvenile cases can be handled formally. Severity is a determining factor in whether a juvenile is offered an informal agreement or sentenced formally. If the case is handled formally, the juvenile may be put in a juvenile holding facility. Bond is placed on a juvenile who is not placed in a holding facility to guarantee appearance in court. When a juvenile is placed in a detention center, a hearing must be held within twenty-four hours of placement to determine if the juvenile's placement should be continued in the detention facility or if he or she should be released on bond.

Once a decision has been made, the next step for the juvenile, whether he or she is held within the detention facility or not, is a formal hearing. At this formal hearing, all parties will discuss the prior record of the juvenile, the seriousness of the offense, and the effectiveness of prior rehabilitative treatment. Two options arise from this formal hearing. If the formal hearing decides that the seriousness of the offense, combined with the failure of rehabilitative treatments, and an extensive prior history warrant a more serious handling of the case, a waiver petition is presented at a hearing and the juvenile is sent to adult court. Depending on the charges and the severity, the juvenile may be able to choose a plea agreement or may face prison time.

For a juvenile to be tried in adult court, he or she must be over the age of fourteen and the delinquent act must be equal to a felony if the juvenile were an adult. During the hearing in which the waiver petition is presented, the juvenile's parent or guardian and attorney must be notified that the waiver will be presented. In many states, once a juvenile is tried in adult court, he or she will be tried for any subsequent offenses in adult court.[17] Since the beginning of the crack cocaine epidemic that increased gun violence, especially juvenile gun violence, and the number of juveniles being arrested for drugs, states have made it easier for prosecutors to transfer cases to adult courts. Approximately six thousand cases were moved from juvenile court to adult courts in 2010; the majority of these were personal and property offenses.[18] Juvenile courts have shown a bias in transferring minority boys to adult courts for adult sentencing.[19]

The other option at the formal hearing is to recommend the juvenile for an adjudicatory hearing. The adjudicatory hearing is the actual trial in a juvenile case. During the hearing, a judge will listen to the evidence and decide if a juvenile is guilty. To find a juvenile guilty, the charges must be proven beyond a reasonable doubt. There is no jury in a juvenile case. Juveniles facing an adjudicatory hearing have the right to have a lawyer, witnesses, and cross-examination of witnesses, and the ability to avoid self-incrimination; these rights are similar to those that adults have in court. If the juvenile is found guilty of the charges, the adjudicatory hearing may be held over until the next day so that the judge is able to conduct a disposition hearing.

A disposition hearing requires that the judge have all the prior information on the juvenile, including personal history; prior offenses; education level; mental, social, and emotional levels; social interactions; home life; and completed treatments. With this information, the judge will determine what type of corrective action will be taken with the juvenile. Corrective actions include counseling, community service, restitution, rehabilitation, and incarceration in a detention center or a juvenile correctional facility. Once the juvenile has completed his or her time in the location deemed appropriate by the judge, he or she is provided a probation officer who checks in on the juvenile and ensures that he or she is following the terms of release and staying out of further trouble.

Unlike adult criminal records, juvenile records are expunged after the juvenile turns nineteen or five years from his or her last visit to juvenile court. However, there are exceptions; if the juvenile has committed a felony, traffic violation, or been identified as a child in need of services (CHINS), those designations follow a juvenile into adult life. CHINS is a designation that is assigned to a juvenile who is beyond the control of his or her parents or guardian, or absent without consent from home, a care facility, a crisis center, or a court-ordered placement and has a drug addiction or is a danger to the community.[20]

With an emphasis on creating safer schools through SROs, metal detectors, searches, surveillance, and a variety of other options, schools have begun to preemptively target students they believe might cause problems. This preemptive targeting is called *preventative detention* and has emerged in schools as a tool to prevent major problems by removing students deemed dangerous.[21] Ronnie Casella, in his study, found that this perceived dangerousness targets minority boys for the way they dress, talk, act, their home lives, friendships, and attitudes; only occasionally is the designation based on actual medical diagnosis or prior behavior.[22] In the past, this behavior could be harmful to the student in the form of increased risk of suspension. Today, targeting perceived dangerousness means that a student can be placed in an alternative setting, limiting his or her ability to receive an education.

Facing pressure from parents and school boards, many schools have chosen to take the safest route by using a proactive response. While it would seem like a smart decision to anticipate and avoid problems before they become an issue, human nature is rarely so easy to predict, especially with tweens and teens. The problem with attempting to predict is not in the attempt, it is in the actual prediction. When we predict that a student will become violent, how much of that does the student feel? When a student is violent, is he or she simply living up to an expectation or does the student truly have a problem? Either way, by choosing to punish the student, we place the blame solely on one person, the student. But what if we our expectations are as much to blame as the student's behavior?

There are no easy answers to these questions; however, there is a direction that we definitely need to avoid. Bringing more law enforcement into schools is not a way to help students who break school policies. Juveniles who become involved in the juvenile justice system rarely have a bright future in front of them once they are labeled a troublemaker. Many already come from troubled homes and rarely have positive influences in their lives. Since juvenile justice systems vary across the fifty states, there is no national rate of juvenile recidivism. This is stunning. If there is no recidivism data collected, how do we know if our juvenile system is working? Could it be possible that our schools are helping to feed a broken system?

The reality is that the discipline policies and juvenile justice systems within our schools need a massive overhaul. While installing cameras, metal detectors, and police officers in schools gives the appearance and illusion of creating a safe environment, it is usually a mirage. Take for instance a 2014 school stabbing at Franklin Regional High School in Pennsylvania; prior to the stabbing, the school had a security officer, students were required to carry clear bags, the school was located near a police station, and the school had in place an antibullying campaign. Yet a student stabbed twenty-one classmates and the security guard in a school rage incident.[23] This ex-student is now charged as an adult for the serious crimes he committed against his classmates. While many may think that this is a fair punishment for a student who hurt so many, what we know about brain development and youth suggest that this student needed help long before he decided to stab his schoolmates. Now, however, the time for help has long passed and his fate is sealed.

While scientists used to believe that juvenile brains were like carbon copies of adult brains, research has proved that this is not the case. Juvenile brains do not begin to mature and decrease in gray matter until the early twenties.[24] The amount of gray matter the brain contains is important; as children our brains are filled with gray matter, this gray matter is filled with neurons, fibers, and support cells that send messages back and forth to each other and various parts of the body.[25] As the brain gets older and matures, the gray matter shrinks and myelin (which improves the speed of the messages sent) increases, making sending messages more efficient and faster; this is why adults can process and think faster than children.[26] Most of the shrinking of the gray matter occurs in the teenage years; this means that juvenile brains function like adults in emotional and intellectual abilities, but are child-like in controlling impulse responses.[27] These impulse responses are why juveniles are more likely to engage in risky behaviors and are not able to understand or discern the full repercussions of an action.

Research on juvenile brains is still an ongoing process. As technology advances, more breakthroughs about how juveniles think and process information will be made. This research should influence how schools and court systems derive their policies and procedures in relationship to punishment. Sadly, this will likely not be the case. Our society is a punitive society; we firmly believe that punishment sends the appropriate message about the behavior that will be tolerated and the behavior that will not be tolerated. When we combine this mentality toward punishment with juveniles who may recognize wrong from right, but are not able to fully comprehend the magnitude of their actions or even control their actions, we send forth a message to that youth that they must be inherently bad. Remember, juvenile brains are like adult brains in intellect and emotional capabilities, juveniles understand and feel like adults do. However, what juveniles cannot do is control their responses as well as adults.

This lack of control can account for juveniles who have lashed out at classmates who have bullied them, teased them, or hurt them; those being hurt lack impulse control. However, our schools and court systems view this lashing out as an inherent flaw in the juvenile, he must be punished before he can harm or hurt others. Suddenly the juvenile goes from being a student at school with a bright future to a convicted felon in prison with no future. The entire direction of the student's life has been altered without his or her conscious knowledge.

This leaves schools and juvenile justice systems with one major question: How can we fix our policies to better serve the juveniles within the system? How I wish this was the question that schools and juvenile systems were asking. Sadly, these two systems believe that the current way they handle issues is acceptable. While schools may state that they are looking for more effective ways to promote school safety, few venture beyond the newest trends or latest demands. This is why SROs, cameras, metal detectors, uniforms, clear bags, and strong discipline policies have increased in school districts; they are the newest and easiest ways to implement trends in school safety. The same goes for juvenile justice systems; it is easy to make a juvenile do community service, attend counseling, or pay a fine. Change is hard, time-consuming, and messy; it requires dedication, perseverance, and courage.

Until schools and juvenile justice systems are willing to change policies that discipline youth, our schools will continue to be at risk for violence. When we can teach juveniles how to handle anger, hurt, frustration, happiness, isolation, and loneliness, then we will have truly safe schools. Yes, it is one more responsibility to be shouldered by schools, but it may be one of our most important responsibilities. When schools were given the legal responsibility of acting *in loco parentis,* or in place of the parent, we were given the ability to teach, discipline, and succeed along with our students. Occasionally, firm hands and discipline are needed to guide a student, but we have come to rely on discipline as a way to control our juveniles.

I would like to wrap this chapter up by leaving you with a story. I asked a friend about the first time she remember an incident that required the police to respond at her school. My friend painted a vivid picture of her ninth grade social studies classroom. She sat in the second row closest to the wall in a classroom that contained one window, cream-colored walls, and a white ceiling. The teacher, a veteran social studies teacher known for her no-nonsense attitude and tough demeanor, ran the classroom with an iron fist. My friend described her classmates as some of the kids known to cause problems for teachers with their talking and behavior. She distinctly remembers during a class on the American Civil War, three police officers stormed into the classroom, grabbed one of the students by his shirt collar, and dragged him out of the classroom. That student did not reappear again until the next school year. In a small school like hers, that student had suddenly received a label that branded him an outcast from his peers and a problem for the school. She recounted to me that although the student reappeared for the first few weeks of class the following year, he soon disappeared again and never returned. She often wonders what happened to her classmate and where he ended up. How many students are lost? Where do they go? What can we do to help?

NOTES

1. S. Bilchik, *Promising Strategies to Reduce Gun Violence* (Washington, D.C.: Office of Juvenile Justice and Delinquency Program, 1999), retrieved from http://www.ojjdp.gov/pubs/gun_violence/173950.pdf.

2. M. Planty and J. Truman, "Firearm Violence, 1993–2011," *Bureau of Justice Statistics,* 2013, retrieved from http://www.bjs.gov/content/pub/pdf/fv9311.pdf.

3. S. Brock, A. Nickerson, and M. Serwacki, "Youth Gun Violence Fact Sheet," *National Association of School Psychologists,* 2013, retrieved from http://www.nasponline.org/resources/crisis_safety/Youth_Gun_Violence_Fact_Sheet.pdf.

4. Planty and Truman, "Firearm Violence, 1993–2011."

5. "Federal Law on Guns in Schools," Law Center to Prevent Gun Violence, 2012, http://smartgunlaws.org/federal-law-on-guns-in-schools/.

6. Goss v. Lopez 419 U.S. 565 (1975).

7. Ibid.

8. Ibid.

9. "Are You Facing a Suspension or Expulsion?" *Kids Legal,* retrieved from http://www.kidslegal.org/are-you-facing-suspension-or-expulsion.

10. National Association of School Resource Officers, retrieved from https://nasro.org/.

11. Ibid.

12. B. Brown, "Understanding and Assessing School Police Officers: A Conceptual and Methodological Comment," *Journal of Criminal Justice* 34 (2006): 591–604.

13. Ibid.

14. B. Raymond, "Assigning Police Officers to Schools," Center for Problem-Oriented Policing, 2010, retrieved from http://www.popcenter.org/Responses/school_police/print/.

15. Ibid.

16. Ibid.

17. "Juvenile Justice: A Century of Change," *Juvenile Justice Bulletin,* 1999, retrieved from https://www.ncjrs.gov/pdffiles1/ojjdp/178995.pdf.

18. C. Puzzanchera and C. Robson, "Delinquency Cases in Juvenile Court, 2010," *Juvenile Offenders and Victims: National Report Series Fact Sheet,* 2014, retrieved from http://www.ojjdp.gov/pubs/243041.pdf.

19. M. C. Young and J. Gainsborough, "Prosecuting Juveniles in Adult Court: An Assessment of Trends and Consequences," The Sentencing Project, 2000, retrieved from http://www.prisonpolicy.org/scans/sp/juvenile.pdf.

20. "Children in Need of Services (CHINS) Petition," Kitsap County, retrieved from http://www.kitsapgov.com/juv/Non-Offender/CHINS.htm.

21. R. Casella, "Punishing Dangerousness through Preventive Detention: Illustrating the Institutional Link between School and Prison," *New Directions for Youth Development* 99 (2003): 55–70.

22. Ibid.

23. G. Botelho and I. Rande, "Complaint: School Stabbing Suspect Said, 'I Have More People to Kill,'" *CNN Justice,* April 25, 2014, retrieved from http://www.cnn.com/2014/04/25/justice/pennsylvania-school-stabbing/.

24. "The Teen Brain: Still Under Construction," National Institute of Mental Health, 2011, retrieved from http://www.nimh.nih.gov/health/publications/the-teen-brain-still-under-construction/index.shtml.

25. Ibid.

26. Ibid.

27. Ibid.

TEN

Our Future

The words that constantly haunt me were told to me by an inmate: "I wish I would have known to stay in school. If I had stayed in school, I might not be here. I wish I could tell all these kids to stay in school. Staying in school is the best way to stay outta here."[1] I think about those words every time I sit down to write, read, research, or speak at a conference. I think about what a difference someone, anyone, might have made if we had stopped punishing and started listening, but at this point, I am powerless to change his current situation. However, I hope that I can make a difference for the next student. Hence the reason for this book.

This book shines a harsh light on the realities of schools and prisons. The truth is, these two institutions are not as far apart as we would like to imagine. Our schools are not gleaming beacons of light, set high upon a hill, where only the best and brightest minds go to achieve enlightenment. It is simply not true. As much as we would like to pretend that every child who attends school is there to learn and achieve to his or her potential, it simply cannot happen. Too many things stand in some children's way.

For some children, the first challenge is even getting to school. A friend of mine worked as an elementary principal in inner-city Atlanta for several years. He told me stories of walking young students home in the evening because they were too scared to walk home on their own. In the mornings, he would meet the same group of students at a relatively safe corner and walk them to school. If he did not walk them to school, they would not attend because they were too scared to traverse their own neighborhoods to risk coming to school. For some students, getting to school proves to be the challenge, but for others, it is what is inside the school that is even more challenging.

Forget the academics for a moment. We know that all students have the potential for some type of learning. Let us look at the social aspect. Navigating the perils of the school world is a challenge. Think back to chapter 6 on cliques. Plotting a course through that mess sounds a lot like wading through shark-infested waters with a gaping wound. Everyone is waiting to find something to pounce on, whether it be the pimples on a student's nose, second-hand clothes because money is tight, or a lisp. Finding a friendly face can be a real challenge. Let us tie that in with what we learned about the juvenile brain in the end of chapter 9. The juvenile brain has a hard time with impulse control, so when a student is constantly being rejected, picked on, or bullied, it is a bit easier to understand why he or she may lash out. One fight, maybe two, and suddenly this student is labeled a problem. This student is the kid no one wants in class because he or she is surly, bad-tempered, and aggressive.

So what happens next? That student makes the teacher's life harder. The student is constantly a problem in class, never does homework, and is always one step away from doing something to irritate, aggravate, annoy, or scare the teachers. To avoid this, the teachers go on hyper-alert. They watch this student's every move like a hawk watches a mouse. Teachers have their eyes on every step the student takes. Sooner or later, they will catch the student doing something bad. It is in the name of safety, they claim, but really, they just want the student out of their hair. He or she is a pain.

Finally, they catch the student doing something atrocious. He or she is taken to the principal and suspended with intent to expel. The teachers breathe a sigh of relief. The student is gone, someone else's problem now, and they go back to their classrooms feeling better, safer, and somewhat justified that their watching paid off. They tell themselves it is normal, okay even, because some kids just are not cut out to make it in school. The student will find something or go to jail. Either way, it is no longer their problem.

However, this is not true. That student is out of sight, out of mind, but he or she is still a problem. Everyone pays taxes. Guess where a portion of that tax money goes? If you guessed prisons, you would be correct. Approximately 45 billion dollars in federal tax money goes to fund state prisons.[2] Therefore, in the end, even though we no longer have to put up with that student being a pain in class or pay for the student's spot in the education world, we now have to pay to house him or her in prison. There is no blame being cast here; everyone is human, and we are taught from a young age that those who break the rules should be punished. It is a reaction that has become so ingrained it seems natural.

Recently, I was sitting in a leadership seminar with a group of twenty people. We had all taken the Myers Briggs Type Indicator (MBTI) to give us deeper insight into our personalities. Once we received our results and went over the types, the instructor asked a question of us. The question our facilitator asked, and how one of my classmates answered, stopped me in my tracks. The facilitator asked us how our personality types may have unknowingly had a negative influence on people with whom we worked. One of my classmates, a former teacher, raised her hand in concern.

She had found out that she was an extrovert with introverted feelings. Basically, that means that she is an exuberant person, who lives life in the moment, finding true enjoyment and energy in people, but that she feels stifled by rules and instead focuses on meeting the needs of individuals. While this would not normally seem like a problem, especially for a teacher, she brought up the idea of how her introverted students must have felt when she encouraged them to learn loudly and interact socially. While *introverted* is often taken to mean *shy,* that is really a misnomer. Extroverted people draw energy from being surrounded by people; introverted people draw energy from within themselves. This sometimes means that introverted students may try to isolate themselves to draw energy and listen to themselves.

In her moment of revelation, my classmate realized that while her teaching style may have been incredibly successful for the majority of her students, for one third to one half of her students, her teaching style may have been detrimental. At that moment, I myself had a revelation. While no personality test is perfect, most of the top one hundred Fortune 500 companies require that their employees take the MBTI or something similar. The purpose for many companies is to make their employees aware of what type of personality they have and how their personality interacts with others, and to try to create more cohesive teams. Why do we not have teachers taking personality type indicator tests and then teaching them how their personalities and learning styles may be similar or different from the personalities and learning styles of their students? Why are we not trying to make classrooms the best teams possible?

Along those same lines and within this same leadership seminar, we discussed strengths and weaknesses. Beyond the superficial, I had never really thought about my strengths and weaknesses. I have always hated mathematics. It was probably the one subject that gave me the hardest time in school. In my mind, it was harder than learning a foreign language. I could never seem to get the numbers to work out in the correct way. My report cards would be filled with As and Bs until it came to mathematics, then I would normally barely squeak by with a C. So what did my parents choose to do? They chose to have me focus on mathematics. I spent long hours at the kitchen table doing repeat math problems trying to figure out how I could solve for x in one equation or y in another. The worst questions were word questions. I thought it was a cruel joke that someone had taken my best subject (reading/English) and combined it with my worst subject.

So I struggled. I felt inadequate. I hated it. I stewed, and I felt bad about myself. How could I be so good in English and reading, but fail so miserably in math? Was I broken? Dumb? Why could my brain not comprehend these simple numbers? I spent hours trying to get better at math, for what purpose? I am still trying to figure that out. I went to college and majored in Secondary English with a minor in Communications. I chose a degree that mirrored my strengths. I have a way with words, and I love to read. It is my strength. During this seminar, our instructor asked us a pointed question. After all the hours spent trying to improve our weaknesses, were we really any better at our weakness? My answer was a definitive no. I can do enough math to balance my checkbook and know a bit about statistics; however, math still gives me a massive headache and makes me feel inadequate. I am fortunate enough that I am able to focus on what I am strong in and be successful at it.

So, here's a thought for you to ponder. Why do we force so many students to focus on their weaknesses? I understand the need to be well rounded, but at what point does trying to be well rounded take a backseat to frustration, anger, hopelessness, misery, and self-loathing? My answer was ninth grade. I had started really struggling with math in fifth grade. Turned out, I needed glasses to see the board, but we did not find that out until almost the end of the year. During that year, I got yelled at for copying problems down wrong and getting bad grades in math. That started my hatred of the subject of math.

By ninth grade, I never wanted to see another math problem again, but that was a fanciful wish because the state of Ohio requires that every student have four years of math to graduate. So I suffered through Algebra I (who came up with the brilliant idea to ruin letters like that), Algebra II (when you do not understand Algebra I, Algebra II is not any better), Geometry (slightly better), and Trigonometry (it was torture). I made it through those and graduated, but to say those classes were hard is an understatement. I used to dread going. Might it have been different if we had found out I needed help seeing sooner? Possibly, but we will never know.

I spent many hours trying to improve one of my weaknesses and still today, it is barely passable and it will never be a strength. I have finally made peace with that and find ways to work around it. I have a great accountant. I keep bank records on a spread sheet. I enlist number-savvy people to help with my research. Today, I wish that all those hours I had spent working on math, I had instead used to fine-tune my strengths.

So what does this mean for our students and ourselves? First, stop focusing and listening to all the criticisms and the weaknesses; we are not perfect, but we are perfectly flawed. For our students, we need to be able to strike a balance between trying to expose them to all the material and forcing them to concentrate on a weakness. It is no wonder that so many students are frustrated by school, especially if they are constantly forced to work on their weakest subjects repetitively. Not every student is going to become a mathematics professor, but all students need a rudimentary knowledge of how to balance their checkbook and keep a budget. Do not force those kids who struggle to become experts. Adequate is enough. Second, for our teachers, stop listening to how awful everyone thinks we are. Yes, we all have things we excel at and things that we are flat out awful at; this is okay.

However, we must be aware of what we do poorly and attempt to do our best, while acknowledging that we are lacking. To make up for this lack in quality, however, hone your strength and do it with pride and vigor. Use your strengths to your advantage, but be aware of your flaws. Think about how much stronger and more amazing you could be if you spent time honing your strengths rather than working toward becoming mediocre on your weaknesses. Teach your students by example; teach them to be proud of their strengths and aware of their weaknesses. Do we not empower kids when we point out what they do well versus when we constantly critique them for what they do wrong? Most students are well aware of their shortcomings long before they are pointed out by a teacher. I would rather hear compliments, constructive criticism, and do work in areas where I am strong than receive constant berating on areas where I am weak. I know where I am weak, so there is no need to keep reminding me.

This mentality is the same for teachers and students. Open the newspaper on any given day and there is an article about how poorly teachers and schools are doing. It is a sore spot already; let us instead focus on what we are doing right. This is the same with troubled students' behavior. They know that they have problems, they know they are struggling; let us focus on what they do well. For example, graffiti artists are a prime example. I have been in a few large cities, walking around before a conference, and have strolled past school age kids cutting class to write on the sides of buildings with spray paint. *Write* is probably the wrong word because writing brings to mind the print on this page, dull, somewhat boring, uniform, and not unique.

Graffiti is art, destructive art, but art nonetheless. So why is the kid cutting class to paint on the side of a building with a can of spray paint (which can get him arrested), when there is a good chance that his school could offer him opportunities to paint with water-based paint, oils, chalk, pen, pencil, or any other medium? The answer to the question lies in the government's focus on testing in areas like mathematics, science, and language arts. Instead of allowing schools to include students' natural strengths and talents in the school day, like art or music, the focus has been placed on test scores. Our strict system of education has removed the personal strength of creativity from our students.

So because that student's passion is not aligned with our strict belief in what education is and looks like, if that student is caught skipping, he is penalized at school. When he has violated school rules enough times, he is removed. We have started down a slippery slope. Schools claim to try to have safeguards in place to help these students. Guidance counselors are one of these safeguard measures; however, their numbers are dwindling.

My mother is one of those contributing to the growing number of guidance counselors leaving the field of counseling. After thirty-nine years as a guidance counselor, she is leaving her job. She loves her job with a passion and the students love her; however, the Ohio Teachers Retirement system is changing and she stands to lose quite a bit if she stays. She has seen at least three generations of students, their parents, and sometimes even grandparents go through her school district. Everywhere we go, we are sure to run into a former student who tells me glowing stories of how my mother helped him or her through the school years. Her specialty is special education. She knows it inside-out and upside-down and probably backward. She really cares about students in a way that makes them feel like her own kids.

In addition to the retirement system changing, her administration is young, hip, and new-fangled; they no longer like the old ways. There is a clash between the changing of the guard. I ponder this clash, since I am one of the new guards. In her defense, while she may have a hard time adjusting to the new ways, she has probably forgotten more on special education and counseling that I have ever learned. Her knowledge and experience is vast, yet her administration treats her like a poor relic, barely useful. Here, I think, is where we have a problem.

New teachers, administrators, and others (counselors, etc.) come into a school with grandiose plans and new ideas, excited and willing to try innovations. In their schools, they often encounter the older, wiser, more experienced teachers. These new teachers sometimes see the older teachers as stagnant, unyielding, unwilling to change, and stubborn, and bemoan the older teachers' existence to friends, other young colleagues, and whoever will listen. That clash is part of the problem; it further divides and destroys the education profession. A camaraderie needs to form; older teachers have the wisdom, experience, and knowledge that come with years spent in a classroom, while younger teachers have the drive, innovation, and new information to share.

Yet it is not just this clash between the old and new that causes valuable information and experiences to be lost. Budget cuts have played a crucial role in driving counselors and others out of the field of education. When the senior counselor whom my mother had worked with for twenty-three years retired, for an entire year, my mother was required to schedule, counsel, administer state tests, perform special education testing, distribute scholarships, help with college and technical applications, and complete a multitude of other tasks for a high school of five hundred with only a secretary and a substitute guidance counselor. After a stressed-out and frazzled year, her school finally hired another counselor who was brand new. While it relieved some of the burden, like any other job, it takes approximately three years for a guidance counselor to learn and feel fully comfortable with his or her responsibilities.

So as the summer winds down and I watch my mother prepare for her last year as a guidance counselor, I reflect on the thousands of stories I have heard from her on current and former students. Stories that range from simple things like helping a student fill out an application for a scholarship so he or she could attend college to the stories that touch your heart, like arranging for a free graduation photograph for a student who was the first in his family to graduate, but too poor to purchase a photo of his big day. She told me that the tears in his eyes and the happiness on his face when she handed him his diploma and the photo made her day. He is now a success story, thanks to his own hard work and my mother's guidance. However, at-risk students across the country are losing their guidance counselors or only have burned-out and over-worked guidance counselors. I worry about my mother's school. There will be one counselor there when she leaves, but will that counselor fill her spot? If not, what happens to those students who teeter on the brink? How will the other counselor find time to do it all in an already overflowing system?

For too many students, this is already their reality. Schools are facing huge budget cuts that have forced them to strip away many of their safeguards, including counselors and secondary help. Even educational programs like kindergarten have been cut in some schools. Even though school violence rates are falling, it should not surprise us when something bad happens at school, since the services that help these at-risk students are being cut. Guidance counselors, school psychologists, and supplemental school personnel are being cut or not hired as schools have tried to make up for budget deficits. This means that students who would be referred to a counselor at the first hint of trouble are not seeing a counselor until it is normally too late. The average guidance counselor's student caseload for the 2010–2011 school year was 471.[3] Some states, like Arizona (861), California (1,016), and Minnesota (782) are almost three and half times the recommended ratio of 250 students to one guidance counselor.[4]

It is not hard to see, then, how schools have turned to other sources to keep schools secure. It is cheaper, due to grants and other monetary options, to employ a school security officer rather than to employee a guidance counselor. According to a presentation done by the nonprofit organization WestEd, there is over 150 million dollars in federal monies available to school districts to defray the cost of hiring a school resource officer (SRO).[5] While guidance counselors counsel students, giving them a place to voice their frustrations, concerns, fears, worries, anger, and other emotions, followed by suggestions or recommendations for more help when students present more severe issues, SROs handle situations in a much different way. While SROs attempt to use the triangulated model of teacher, counselor, and law enforcer that was discussed in chapter 9, their first and foremost duty is as a law enforcement officer.

Students, therefore, are wary about discussing their personal lives with an SRO, especially if the student feels that he, she, or a family member could get into serious trouble with the issues that need discussed. This wariness can be exacerbated when SROs are forced to remove and arrest students for school violations, which can make it hard to build bonds that foster relationships that are crucial for opening the lines of communication. Instead, SROs create atmospheres that provide a feeling of safety and security, but offer little in the way of creating trust and openness. WestEd reviewed the research conducted on SROs and created a list of pros and cons. On the positive side, SROs were found to increase safety, improve perceptions of the school, reduce offenses committed at school, and enhance the reputation of the school.[6] Negative things associated with SROs included increased referrals for breaking school policies, climate effects, increased distrust, and disparity.[7] A definite answer on the effectiveness of SROs is still being studied, currently; the research can be interpreted to support either side.

While SROs may be a positive addition for schools that can support both an SRO and a guidance counselor, SROs as a replacement for a guidance counselor can be a poor decision. When lines of communication are closed to students, whether it be a perceived closure or a true closure, bad consequences can happen. I always picture youth, especially young teens, as bottle rockets. They are full of emotions, passion, and energy, but they sometimes lack focus, direction, and control and in the confusing and consuming world of school; an explosion is sometimes imminent. Since most youth lack the ability to control their impulses and they are constantly subjected to criticism, ridicule, pressure, and other emotions and stressors, without a trusted confidant, youth can explode.

These explosions can range in kind and severity. Some youth handle their stresses and emotions by taking it out on their own bodies in the form of eating disorders, self-mutilation, or compulsive or control behaviors. Other youth handle stress by taking it out on those who torment them; this can involve anything from a verbal altercation to fighting, and even more serious actions like school shootings or stabbings. After a major event, or even a minor issue, parents, community members, friends, and others are all left wondering about what the youth was thinking and why the action occurred. When no counselor is present or the counselor is mired down, the warning signs are missed and there is no one to turn to for insight.

Support and treatment can be sought in the mental health community by youth and their parents. If a student is under the age of eighteen, a parent or guardian needs to provide consent for outside, private counseling. Sadly, however, unless the former student is wealthy enough to be able to pay for a private mental health specialist, the public system is overtaxed. The National Association of Social Workers does not have a recommended ratio of cases per social worker and little information is available on national averages statistics.

However, what is known is that social workers and others are overwhelmed with cases and paperwork. Since each case requires its own specific set of paperwork, goals, plans, and notes, social workers cram their days and nights full of seeing patients and attempting to fill in and file the appropriate paperwork. Even the most conscientious and adept social worker can let people slip through the cracks or miss subtle changes in clients as they move to the next case. Numerous studies have shown that the number involves the one preventable reason for social workers leaving the profession involves high numbers of caseloads.[8] It is estimated that in a clinical social work model the average number of clients to social workers is 365 to 1; this is just a rough estimate, and in some areas it may be higher or lower.[9]

If a person is fortunate enough to be counseled by a social worker, then other issues arise. Is the client in a position where he or she can continue permanent counseling or is he or she transient (e.g., homeless, low-income, etc.)? If the client is prescribed medication, can he or she afford to pay for it, even with the help offered for those in low-income brackets? Will the client continue to take the medication that is prescribed, or once he or she begins to act "normal" will the client believe he or she is cured? Unlike in school, where the behavior of students who have issues can be monitored and checked on, once they are out of school, the onus falls on the former student, who can be ill-prepared to deal with this responsibility.

People who are not fortunate enough to see a counselor or who see a counselor but are then either transient or cannot afford the price of medicine often turn to self-medication. *Self-medication* refers to the practice of using alcohol or illegal drugs as a form of medication to mask, dull, or drown out the issues that are plaguing the person. If he or she is fortunate enough to not have a prior record from high school, this person may be able to slip past the notice of the police until the habit leads him or her to more destructive behavior. The behavior of those who have a prior record rarely goes unnoticed and they are incarcerated quickly.

A Department of Justice Bureau of Justice Statistics study released in 2006 found that 56 percent of state inmates, 45 percent of federal inmates, and 64 percent of jail inmates had mental health issues.[10] These percentages seem perfectly reasonable when viewed in light of the top three types of incarceration at the state and federal levels. At the state level in 2010, the top three types of violations for inmates were violence, property crimes, and drugs; at the federal level in 2011, the top three were drugs, public order (immigration and weapons), and violence.[11]

Once incarcerated, inmates find themselves subjected to routines and spaces that are similar to their former institutions, like bells signaling when to move, attendance counts, uniforms, guards who monitor behavior, meetings with specialists, documentation, and other routines and policies. Inmates also find they are faced with social situations similar to those found in their prior schools. Gangs, similar to the high school cliques, abound in prison, searching for new people to recruit as members. Guards, like teachers, have personality styles that clash with certain inmates, creating friction and tension. Violence, always a danger in both institutions, happens with more frequency inside prison walls. I was once told by a former teacher turned prison guard that the three biggest problems in schools (cell phones, violence, and drugs) were the same three biggest problems in prison. I found that ironic even before I had truly begun my research into the similarities of prisons and schools.

To me, then, the problem is cyclical. Students who have problems and get in trouble in school are mostly the same adults who get in trouble in society and are incarcerated. Then the cycle begins again with their children. It is estimated that approximately 52 percent of state inmates and 63 percent of federal inmates left an estimated 1.7 million children, or 2.3 percent of the U.S. population under the age 18, at home when they went to prison. [12] At one point, it was assumed that most incarcerated parents were fathers; however, since 1991, the rate of maternal incarceration has increased 131 percent, while the rate of paternal incarceration has increased by 77 percent. [13] The problem that has arisen with skyrocketing rates of maternal incarceration is that 42 percent of these women were the sole parent before their incarceration. [14] For mothers, this has left the care of raising minor children in the hands of grandparents; for incarcerated fathers, minor children are left to be raised with their mothers. [15]

Research conducted by several different entities has shown that these children have more problems in school than children of nonincarcerated parents. It has been difficult to narrow down the cause of these problems to parental incarceration, especially since so many other factors are often in the picture. However, parental incarceration affects family stability, the behavior, and emotional well-being of the child, and financial solvency. [16] Some studies have even postulated a correlation between incarcerated parents and a child's behavior, academic performance, and mental health. [17]

Black children are seven and a half times more likely than White children to have a parent who is incarcerated, while Hispanic children are two and a half times more likely than White children to have an incarcerated parent. [18] These children can be at further risk. An overview of the research prepared by the Annie E. Casey Foundation, which is dedicated to improving the futures of susceptible children and families in the United States, theorized that children of incarcerated parents were six times more likely than their peers to be imprisoned as adults. [19] While this is just a theory and actual evidence is slim, it is a sobering thought to ponder.

While research might say that the evidence to support the increased association between incarcerated parents and their children's future incarceration is only a correlation and not causation, I am a firm believer in the old adage that where there is smoke, there is fire. This may seem strange coming from a doctoral student who was taught the value of causation. Currently, there are too many factors that cannot be separated out that affect a child's life for researchers to find a definite link between an incarcerated parent and a child's future risk of incarceration. Nonetheless, research methods are improving daily, with new instruments being developed alongside new methods of data collection and analysis. I believe that one day, we may be able to find a causal link. Until that day, however, I believe that we need to work with the correlations that we have, especially if we can save just one child from going to prison.

I have thought long and hard, spoken with numerous people, conducted hours of research, and spent many sleepless nights thinking about how I wanted to end this book. In my dreams, I suggest the perfect solution that can be implemented flawlessly in schools across the nation, keeping every troubled student in school, allowing them to graduate and go on to lead successful lives. Alongside this dream, I magically manage to revamp the entire prison system, creating an institution where therapy, rehabilitation, and learning are the focal points. However, reality is harsh and human nature dictates that for some, therapy, rehabilitation, and learning will not help. Therefore, I would like to end this book by asking you some hard questions and challenging you to examine your own practices.

Here's the first set of questions I believe we all need to ask ourselves:

- Are we using the best possible practices, policies, and procedures within the spaces we control?
- Have you thought out all of the effects that your rules have on the children, youths, and wards under your control?
- Do we understand the explicit and subtle messages our rules, policies, and practices send to those under our care?
- To those who view our policies, practices, and rules from the outside, do our practices, policies, and rules have subtle or clear biases?
- Are we aware of what these biases mean and do to our students, youths, or wards?

I believe that through a blind ignorance, many of us follow and implement the rules, policies, and practices of those before us without much thought to those we supervise or control. We do it because that is the way it has always been done and it has always worked. However, when we stop and think about whether or not it has always worked, we may find that it has worked for the successful few, but for the majority it has failed.

The second question set I believe we need to ask ourselves are these:

- Do we really care or are we just being politically correct? If it does not affect our kid, is it really important and does it need to be changed?
- Do we care about poor or troubled children or is it out of sight, out of mind?
- Can we step up and take responsibility for all students, without shortchanging other students?

These questions are difficult because no one wants to look politically incorrect. In this era, it is almost a sin to be politically incorrect. However, we use phrases like "best practice" or "statistically significant" and know that the hidden, underlying message is that these practices work best for high-performing, middle-class, White students. Then we implement these practices to improve our schools. Then we wonder why they work so well in those high-performing and middle-class schools, but fail so spectacularly in low socioeconomic schools. We speak in hidden phrases and couched terms, so we never seem politically incorrect, yet all of our talk is a racial doublespeak.

The third set of questions I would like you to ask yourself is based on change:

- Do we really want to change our practices? Do we really believe all students can succeed?
- Are all kids able to learn?
- Can we make our schools places of success for all students?
- What do schools that are successful look like from diverse student viewpoints?

Currently, I get the feeling that very few people believe that schools can be made to help all students succeed. From the current reforms that happen every four years when a new president is elected, I can understand the frustration. In the past twenty years, many educational reforms have been passed by presidential administrations, causing rapid change and little progress.

All of those reforms have focused on the content that schools are supposed to teach. The actual physical aspect of school has changed little since the 1800s. If we are to create a positive and lasting change in education, we need to change the way schools are built, run, and service students. We need a reform plan that will help schools create new and effective policies and practices, as well as the money, space, and time to build and use student-based data to create lessons that engage and teach students. That means that the emphasis on testing and numbers needs to come to a halt.

We have become a society dominated by numbers, tests, and percentages. Learning has become regimented, tightly controlled, and competitive, which harms students and teachers. I am not advocating for no testing. I believe tests serve as an important comparative measure and as a way to check on the gains made by students. However, when students spend at least a month testing out of an approximate nine-month school calendar, we have a serious problem.

My last set of questions to you is of a more personal nature:

- Do you go to work every day believing that you are doing the best job that you can possibly do?
- Or do you trudge into work, dreading the day ahead of you?
- Does your job allow you to showcase your strengths?
- Are you having a positive influence on those you come into contact with every day?

Somewhere, I heard that only 2 percent of people use their strengths at work and are truly happy at their jobs, meaning that 98 percent of us are just in the routine. But I ask that you at least be aware of that and how those feelings you try to hide affect the children, youths, and wards that you control and supervise on a daily basis. Do they feel your hatred, boredom, or disinterest? Do they feel that it is aimed at them? What subtle or explicit messages do your body language, words, facial expressions, and even posture send to those with whom you are in contact?

I then challenge you to try this: Think about your behavior for the next few weeks. After you think and have a rough idea of how others perceive you, change your behavior, even if only for a day. If you are normally grouchy and unhappy going into work, go into work positive and happy for a day. See if you notice changes in how people treat you and how you treat others. My mother said that she went to school each morning with a renewed vow to have a positive influence in the life of at least one student. Even after thirty-nine years, that is still her daily goal.

In the larger picture, however, change needs to occur by changing who is elected to positions of power. Change will not happen if people without educational backgrounds or knowledge are elected to fill the positions that control education. Although the prior three presidents have run on the self-proclaimed title of "education president," none of them had experience or knowledge about the status of education in the United States. Therefore, it is up to those who work in the field every day to speak up and out about their needs, their realities, and their hopes for their schools and students.

While I have asked some difficult questions of you, I still have not supplied an answer to how we create change in these institutions. I believe that real change will be slow in coming because change is scary and painful for many people. Most people are comfortable with routine; therefore, change must come about slowly and individually until the time is right. That is the purpose of the previous questions. If one person at a time slowly becomes aware of how his or her actions affect others in a way that he or she had never previously thought about, and if that person is willing to change himself or herself to create a better environment for everyone, slowly policies, practices, and rules will change to reflect this growing awareness. This slow change is not ideal or even perfect, but it is the one way to create lasting change. This lasting change can be the difference between prison bars or open doors of opportunity for millions of students.

NOTES

1. Conversation with an inmate serving life for murder.
2. J. W. Schoen, "Here's Where Your Federal Income Tax Dollars Go," NBC News, 2012, retrieved from http://www.nbcnews.com/business/economy/heres-where-your-federal-income-tax-dollars-go-f654971.
3. "Student-to-School-Counselor Ratio 2010–2011," American School Counselor Association, retrieved from http://www.schoolcounselor.org/asca/media/asca/home/ratios10-11.pdf.
4. Ibid.
5. Fronius, Guckenburg, Petrosino, "Policing Schools' Strategies to Reduce Crime in Primary and Secondary (K-12) Schools," presented April 5, 2014, at the UCEA conference in Philadelphia, Pennsylvania.
6. Ibid.
7. Ibid.
8. Social Work Policy Institute, "High Caseloads: How Do They Impact Delivery of Health and Human Services?" *Research to Practice Brief*, retrieved from http://www.socialworkpolicy.org/wp-content/uploads/2010/02/r2p-cw-caseload-swpi-1-10.pdf.
9. Wilson, Curtis, Lipke, Bachenski, and Gillian, 2005.
10. J. D. James and L. E. Glaze "Mental Health Problems of Prison and Jail Inmates," *Bureau of Justice Statistics Special Report,* U.S. Department of Justice, retrieved from http://www.nami.org/Template.cfm?Section=Press_September_2006&Template=/ContentManagement/ContentDisplay.cfm&ContentID=38175.
11. E. A. Carson and W. J. Sabol, "Prisoners in 2011," *Bureau of Justice Statistics,* U.S. Department of Justice, 2012, retrieved from http://bjs.gov/content/pub/pdf/p11.pdf.
12. L. E. Glaze and L. M. Maruschak "Parents in Prison and Their Minor Children," *Bureau of Justice Statistics Report,* U.S. Department of Justice, 2008, retrieved from http://www.bjs.gov/content/pub/pdf/pptmc.pdf.
13. Ibid.
14. Ibid.
15. Ibid.
16. S. Christian, "Children of Incarcerated Parents," *National Conference of State Legislatures,* 2009, retrieved from http://www.ncsl.org/documents/cyf/childrenofincarceratedparents.pdf.
17. J. Murray and D. Farrington, "Effects of Parental Imprisonment on Children," in *Crime and Justice: A Review of Research* (Chicago: University of Chicago Press, 2008).
18. Glaze and Maruschak, *Parents in Prison.*
19. C. F. Hairston, *Focus on Children with Incarcerated Parents: An Overview of the Research Literature* (Baltimore: Annie E. Casey Foundation, 2007), retrieved from http://www.f2f.ca.gov/res/pdf/FocusOnChildrenWith.pdf.

Index

teachers in, 4; testing in, 7–8, 9–10;
West in, 6
EHA. *See* Education for the
Handicapped Act
Elementary and Secondary Education
Act (ESEA), 8, 91
ELSA. *See* Employability and Life
Skills Assessment
EMOs. *See* educational management
organizations
Employability and Life Skills
Assessment (ELSA), 45
employment: drugs for, 108; for ex-
inmates, 25–26; prisons and, 39; in
private prisons, 111, 113; strengths
in, 143
ESEA. *See* Elementary and Secondary
Education Act
ethical leadership, 89; development of,
97–98, 98–99; economics of, 90;
NCLB in, 90–91, 91–92, 94–95;
questions for, 141–142
ethics, 89
Ewert, S., 55
expulsion, 120–121, 122–123

families: gangs as, 78, 79; in
punishment history, 16
FAPE. *See* free and appropriate public
education
Faulaau, Mary Kay (Mary Kay
LeTourneau), 34, 41n18
Federal Bureau of Investigation, 23, 79,
96
First Amendment, 34
football, 38
Ford, Gerald, 8–9
forgiveness, 99–100
formal education: definition of, 1, 12n1;
requirement of, 2; Satan related to,
1, 2; in 1700s, 2–3
Fourteenth Amendment, 121
free and appropriate public education
(FAPE), 51–52
funding: for charter schools, 104–105;
in education history, 9, 10

gangs, xii, 80, 83; cliques compared to,
78; cliques' development into,

84–85; colors of, 81, 83; drugs and,
99; economics of, 80; as family, 78,
79; gender and, 78–79; hierarchy
within, 83–84; membership in, 78,
82–83; most dangerous, 79; origins
of, 82; principles of, 84; race related
to, 79, 80; rules for, 79–80; tattoos
for, 83; violence of, 79, 80, 81. *See
also* prison gangs
Garcia, Lorenzo, 95
gender, 63; cliques and, 75; education
history and, 2; gangs and, 78–79
get-tough laws, 23
GFSA. *See* Gun-Free School Act
GFSZA. *See* Gun-Free School Zone Act
Goffman, Erving, 29, 60. *See also* total
institution
Goss v. Lopez (1975), 121
graduation. *See* high school graduation
guidance counselors, 136–138
Gun-Free School Act (GFSA), 117–118
Gun-Free School Zone Act (GFSZA),
118

Hall, Beverly, 94
Harlow, Caroline Wolf, 54
Harvard College, 2
Head Start, 8
high school graduation: economics of,
55; of inmates, 54, 95; race and, 93
high schools, 45–46; in education
history, 4, 6
high-security prisons (penitentiaries),
24
Hispanic boys. *See* African-American
and Hispanic boys
Hoover, J. Edgar, 23
house rules: class rules compared to,
36–37; of total institutions, 36–37
Howard, John, 60
humiliation, 19, 31
Hutcherson, Donald T., 26

IAES. *See* interim alternative education
setting
IDEA. *See* Individuals with Disabilities
Education Act
IDEIA. *See* Individuals with
Disabilities Education Improvement